Coat of Many Colors

EUGENE EOYANG

Coat of Many Colors

Reflections on Diversity by a Minority of One

BEACON PRESS · BOSTON

Beacon Press
25 Beacon Street
Boston, Massachusetts 02108-2892

Beacon Press books
are published under the auspices of
the Unitarian Universalist Association of Congregations.

99 98 97 96 95   8 7 6 5 4 3 2 1

Text design by Wesley B. Tanner, Ann Arbor

Library of Congress Cataloging-in-Publication Data

Eoyang, Eugene Chen.
Coat of many colors: reflections on diversity by a minority of one /
Eugene Eoyang.
p.   cm.
Includes bibliographical references (p.   ) and index.
ISBN 0-8070-0420-0
1. Pluralism (Social sciences)—United States. 2. Immigrants—United
States. 3. Multiculturalism—United States. 4. United States—Race
relations. 5. United States—Ethnic relations.
I. Title.
E184.A1E62   1995
305.8—dc20   94-13421
CIP

To my mother,

Ellen Tsao Eoyang,

who insisted on our coming
to America

Contents

"E Pluribus . . ."

This book started out as another book. At the end of 1989, I presented a talk at the annual meeting of the Modern Language Association entitled "The Semiotics of 'We'," which seemed to strike a nerve with some, and to strike a chord with others (chapter 1 is based on that talk). On that occasion, one critic left me dumbfounded; he said that, although he admired the way I presented my ideas, he disagreed with everything I had to say. Why didn't he walk out in disgust, I asked myself? Or, if curiosity had compelled him to stay, why didn't he leave the premises without a word, dismissing me and my ideas. On the contrary, he insisted on remonstrating with me in a friendly, insistent, almost conspiratorial way (ignoring a small crowd that was collecting behind him to offer the usual—brief— commendations). He was a teacher of French in Florida, and he couldn't understand why someone of my educational breeding could be so wrongheaded. In the spirit of the occasion, I conceded that I had perhaps exaggerated my point just to elicit a response from the audience. And then it became clear why he insisted on "recuperating" me from the ranks of his opponents: "Don't you realize," he said, "that you're playing into *their* hands?" ("Their," I finally realized, were the unwanted Puerto Ricans, Haitians, and Cubans in Dade County, the Mexicans in southern California and Texas, the vulgar enemies of all that was civilized and cultured.) Ah! I thought, he views me as a wayward elitist, unaccountably misguided—despite the civilized accents of my discourse. In order to cut off his determined recriminations, I allowed him to think that perhaps I had inadvertently played the fool. Yes, I admitted, I hadn't thought about the possibility of being politically co-opted by "them."

That encounter both pleased and depressed me. It pleased me because it was clear that I had somehow unsettled him. I felt a modest triumph in his *not* dismissing what I said out of hand. Yet it depressed me as well because clearly he had not heard a word I had said.

I began thinking about diversity in an almost visceral way. It puzzled me why people forget their diverse origins time and time again. I remember as a public school student in P.S. 173 in New York City being assigned to draw a map of the United States, indicating all the immigrant contributions to American culture. John Jacob Astor, I dimly recall, was designated in the Northwest with a cartoon of a beaver, indicating his early success as a trapper; Thomas Edison was placed in New Jersey with the inevitable icon of a lightbulb. Their ethnic origins were not then specifically clear to me, but I was reminded that they were, in any case, immigrants or descended from immigrants.[1] Even as well intended as that grade school map was, there were egregious omissions: no reference to the Chinese contribution to the transcontinental railroad; no mention of the Spanish element in the culture of the great Southwest or of the Florida peninsula; little if anything, as I recall, of the Scandinavian presence in Minnesota and Wisconsin. Yet what was taught, and presumably learned, a generation ago seems to elude our consciousness. The last thing

---

1. In retrospect, I discover that the Astors were Anglo-Americans and that Edison was born in Milan, Ohio, which—despite the Italian-sounding name of his birthplace—does not make him an immigrant.

I expected was that, thirty years later, I would still be reminding adult audiences in America of lessons I learned in grade school. Perhaps, I thought, they did not have the same teachers I had when they were in grade school. Some of the very guardians of cultural purity were themselves on the perimeters of mainstream culture a generation ago; that, however, did not prevent them from being the more adamant in their defense against cultural contamination. After every wave of immigration, there is always a backlash, a concern about being overrun and overwhelmed (a "Yellow Wave"?); the irony is that the most recent immigrants to settle are often the most intolerant toward the newest wave of immigrants who are about to settle.[2]

I didn't know the ethnic origins of my interlocutor from Florida, but I did ask about the origins of French culture, on which he was, presumably, expert. In the days of the Gauls and the Franks, and before France became a unified country, wasn't early French culture, I asked, something of a hodgepodge? Wasn't France—like every country in the world, including such contrastive cultures as China and the United States—the result of mixtures of races, peoples, and cultures? The raising of the Iron Curtain at the end of the 1980s has reminded us of what we should have known all along, that many nations—the Soviet Union, Yugoslavia, Iran, Iraq, India—are precarious political constructs that are uneasy coalitions of various cultural strains. Almost half a century after the Nazis, have we forgotten the unsupportable and pernicious lie of racial and cultural purity? I

2. Somehow the stability of proportional growth is reassuring, namely, the following excerpt from the 1966 edition of the *Encyclopedia Britannica*, in the entry on the United States: "Between 1910 and 1920 there had been little change in the proportion of non-whites. It was 10.3 in 1920 and 10.2 in both 1930 and 1940, and 10.5 in 1950. The 1960 proportion is still less than that at the beginning of the century, when it was 12.1." It is significant that the most recent backlash against immigrants and against "foreign" influences began in the 1960s.

barely managed to formulate these questions before my interlocutor from Florida changed the subject.

Months later, I came on an article by Robert Reich entitled
"Who Is 'Us'?" published in the January 1990 issue of the
Harvard Business Review. Reich's critique reminds us that even
the notion of corporations as monolithically American is subject
to doubt. Is a corporation that is owned by the Japanese but
staffed by Americans an "American" corporation? What about
corporations in other countries where the principal stockholder
is American. Are they American companies or foreign?

It struck me that the argument for diversity could be made
in a number of other areas, not just in cross-cultural or multicultural studies, but in national histories as well as in the physical
and social sciences. Nature is, as the French would say, *foison-
nant*, almost infinitely various and outlandishly variegated. Recent studies in chaos theory persuade us not to dismiss the
marginal and the indeterminate. Surely evolution theory makes
no sense without a principle of fecund diversity. In a very real
sense, one could say that whatever survives is the result of many
origins and a host of developmental factors.

As a student of literature and language, I am fascinated by the
different nuances attached to cognate words: why is it that *mosaic*,
which was initially accepted as an aesthetically flattering term to
describe fragmentary diversity, is now under attack? Why are
such images as *patchwork quilt*, which was once used to denigrate
the incoherence of a literary work, now seen as symbols of
solidarity (the AIDS quilt doubtless changed our attitude about
images of multiculturalism—if not about AIDS). In the nationwide concern with changing the core curriculum, faculty and
administrators use pejoratives like *smorgasbord* and *hodgepodge*
and *jumble* and *mish-mash* and *chop suey*. But it is also possible to
speak of diversity in neutral or positive terms: *assortment, potpourri, mixture, variety, mélange,* and *medley* come to mind. Well-

orchestrated compositions, involving many different instruments under unified direction playing to a common beat, are called *symphonies*. *Melting pot* used to be positive until Daniel Moynihan and Nathan Glazer taught us to be suspicious of its emphasis on homogenization. *Rainbow*, as Jesse Jackson has demonstrated, is politically viable as well as romantic. There seems to be a subjective Rohrschach quality to diversity: it is whatever one wishes to make of it. "A Frenchman's bouillabaisse is a Spaniard's paella."

So, pondering these concerns about diversity, which revolve around the "e pluribus" ("out of many") theme, I thought to collect a volume of essays from diverse hands—an "e pluribus" on "e pluribus," as it were. But the project was slow, and I grew impatient. In the end, I decided to collect my own essays on diversity, which, I hoped, would offer some variety even if it were from one pen. I decided on a strategy familiar to the traditional Chinese scholar, "To throw out a brick to elicit jade." The proverb, unfortunately, does not translate very well because it makes it appear that, in Chinese conversations and colloquiums, people are throwing brickbats at each other. But there is a metaphoric aptness nevertheless because we do say, "Let me throw out an idea," or, "Let me try this idea out on you." The point of the comparison is that what I offer is a humble brick, but the response—either by way of contradiction or confirmation—is precious jade. It is in the hopes of eliciting this precious jade that I venture forth with these wayward meditations.

Although I have eliminated inevitable repetitions and redundancies, I have not entirely erased the topical and occasional character of those chapters that were originally written in response to invitations to speak. I know that this strategy will "date" the essays (it's interesting how up-to-date one wants to be yet how quickly everything becomes dated). Attention to the exact time and place of these talks, addresses, and speeches is an essential ingredient of active discourse, and I have noted the circumstances of these presentations. Four of the chapters, chapters 7–10, were written after the other pieces were assembled, because they addressed questions that had not been adequately explored in the other expositions.

I do not believe the simplistic view of language as communication, where meaning, like the contents of a container, is to be boxed, shipped, received, unwrapped, and opened, unchanged and intact. I believe that language is the sharing of contexts, and the image that I find more helpful than the encoding-transmission-decoding model of information theorists is that of an electrolytic battery, where the sodium chloride solution is the context, the positive and negative poles are the interlocutors, and the platinum catalyst represents the linguistic, logical, and emotional paradigms of discourse. This model is much more adequate for explaining not only the successes but also the complex failures of language. When language is well used, there is a "current" between the interlocutors; when language fails (as it so often does, even when two people know and use the same language), something is missing, either the right solution ("the context of meaning") or the right catalyst. The occasional nature of these essays is important to their context of meaning. I have adapted them to a (new) reading audience, and I have eliminated the oratorical flourishes that are effective before an immediate audience but that may seem limp to remote, solitary readers. I would ask only that the reader remember the original events that occasioned the "scripts" (meaning both something written as well as a record of an oral presentation) from which these text versions have been prepared.

Finally, a note on terminology.

It is not possible, at least for me, to be absolutely neutral about ethnic labels. *Negro* was considered objectionable by people so designated by whites, and they preferred to call themselves *black* (although some blacks whose skin color is not black may balk at this label as well). *African-American* is now, in some circles, preferred to *Afro-American*—although it sanctifies what most citizens of countries in Africa resent, that is, the monolithic reference to the disparate nations and cultures on that continent as (homogenously) African. Citizens of South Africa are no less African than Nigerians, whatever one's politics, but white South Africans do not come readily to mind when the word *African* is mentioned.

Oriental is now a dated word, which, as Edward Said reminds us, designates anything east of the Suez with one label, thus conflating vastly different civilizations: the Arabs, the Indians, the Chinese, the Japanese, etc. However, in common parlance, at least since the Second World War, *Oriental* usually designates specifically East Asians; very few people refer nowadays to Arabs as Orientals. When I speak here of Chinese, Japanese, and Koreans generically, I will refer to them as *East Asians*, but, when I am characterizing the popular reference to them that may or may not embody prejudice, I shall write *Oriental.* These are slippery terms, and, depending on which group is being addressed, somebody will be offended by whatever term is used. *Asian-American* is hardly more specific than *Oriental,* although it does not have the same ethnocentric nuance: Iraqi-Americans and Iranian-Americans are also Asian-Americans, but one does not immediately identify them that way. Usage and precision often vie with each other in terms of reference, but more precise designations are not always more palatable. The playwright Frank Chin, for example, dislikes the hyphenization of any ethnic designation because it suggests that the members of the group are somehow downgraded as hybrid, belonging neither here nor there. He therefore avoids using *Chinese-American,* favoring, in its stead, the incendiary *Chink* or *Chinaman*—terms that are highly derogatory and reflect regressive denigrations of the Chinese in the United States. Still, as sympathetic as one might be about Chin's concern with hyphens, there is too much negative baggage for many Americans of Chinese descent to accept *Chink* or *Chinaman* as self-designations.

It should also be noted that I use the words *America* and *American* to designate citizens of the United States, even though I am conscious of the inaptness (to say nothing of the ineptness) of these designations, since, terminologically, citizens of all the Americas—North American, Central America, and South America—have a right to call themselves *Americans*.[3]

ACKNOWLEDGMENTS

The impetus for many of the essays in this book came from individuals who invited me to speak on special occasions. I have always believed in occasions and have regretted the denigration of the word *occasional* in English as reflecting something offhand, irregular, and somehow irrelevant. I take occasions seriously, not only because there are heightened expectations at such gatherings, but because the character of the audience and its interests at that moment in history provide the clearest possible focus for a speaker and a writer.

"The Semiotics of 'We': First-Person Pluralities in 'Us'" was the result of a commission by the Ad-Hoc Committee on Foreign Language Programs of the Modern Language Association, which accomplished so much under the dedicated and imaginative leadership of Professor Winfred P. Lehmann of the University of Texas. The piece was subsequently published in the *ADFL Bulletin* (22, no. 1 [Fall 1990]: 29–34). "Taking the 'Foreign' out of Foreign-Language Teaching" emerged from a talk given at the 1988 ADFL Seminar West. I am grateful to Denise Bourassa

3. In chapter 11, I consider and reject some novel, even "nominal," solutions to his problem.

Knight for the initial invitation and to Judith Ginsberg for shepherding the script through publication in the *ADFL Bulletin* (20, no. 2 [January 1989]: 5–10).

Some of the material in "Seeing with Another I: Our Search for Other Worlds" developed out of cross-cultural seminars that I have conducted at the Indiana University School of Business Executive Education Programs since 1986, both in the Professional Manager project and in the Indiana Partnership for Management Development programs. I am indebted to Cam Danielson and John Boquist of the Indiana University School of Business for providing me with a hard-nosed forum in which to temper and refine my notions of cross-cultural understanding. A series of invitations to several New Jersey institutions of higher learning inspired me with the thought that there might be an audience for these musings. I am grateful to David T. Abalos of the New Jersey Department of Higher Education, who invited me to participate in a memorable faculty workshop in the summer of 1989 at the first Multicultural Scholarship Institute, held at Seton Hall University. That led to invitations from Nino Scarpatti to present a multicultural lecture at Trenton State College in March 1990 and from Alene Graham and Melba Ramos to offer a talk at the second statewide Conference on Multicultural Scholarship at Jersey City State College. Portions of "Seeing with Another I" developed out of these presentations. A later version appeared in *An Other Tongue: Essays on Bilingualism and Multiculturalism*, edited by Alfred Arteaga (Durham, N.C.: Duke University Press, 1994). The seeds for "The Complexities of Complexion: The Myths of Skin Color" and "Coat of Many Colors: The Myth of a White America" began to germinate in remarks made at Glassboro State College, when I was invited by Ronald J. Czochor to speak on cultural diversity. "Literati and Illiterati: Continuities in the Oral and Written Traditions" was presented on the campus of Montclair State College at the celebration, on 14 September 1990, of the International Literacy Year. Joseph Brunner and Tina Jacobowitz, cochairs of the conference, were gracious enough to invite me. Through the good offices of Jerry Weiss, the text of that presentation appeared in *Signal* (15, no. 2 [Winter 1991]: 13–18).

Roger Ray, of the Humanities Institute at the University of Toledo, asked me to participate in a series of public humanities programs, "Asia Old and New," a project funded by the National Endowment for the Humanities. "China and the United States: Reflections on the Old and the New" emerged out of my speculations on that occasion. My friend and colleague Ben Brabson was responsible for issuing the invitation that led to "The Three L's: Liberalism, Liberty, and the Liberal Arts," the address that I offered to the inductees of the Gamma Chapter of Phi Beta Kappa in November 1988 at Indiana University.

Many friends and colleagues contributed to these essays. To Allen Winold and Helga Winold, I owe gratitude not only for their friendship but also for their committed and constructive criticism. They have often been my first audience, and, if what I write warrants the interest of the public, it is because it first passed muster with Allen and Helga. To Harry Geduld, who is, wondrously, a friend even as (some might say even though) he is chair of one of the departments in which I hold an appointment, I am indebted for unflagging support, sometimes in the face of significant opposition: he has urged me repeatedly to make a book out of these essays. To other friends who have offered encouragement, help, and criticism—Phyllis Franklin, Win Lehman, John Boening, Carl Ziegler, Sumie Jones, Cam Danielson, John Boquist, Carl and Margot Lenhart, Debbie Struemph, Hans Busch—I can offer only token thanks for their support and their faith in me. I am also indebted to one "Doctor Grammaticus" from "Urbe Angelorum" for pointing out the "rectius loquimur" to me.

And to Patricia Eoyang, who has thought more of me than I have thought of myself, and who has insisted that I share with others part of what I have shared with her over thirty years, no public expression of thanks will be adequate. She reflects the best in me; she is, more than just proverbially, my better half.

Eugene Eoyang
Bloomington, Indiana
May 1994

CHAPTER ONE

The Semiotics of "We":
First-Person Pluralities in "Us"

N-*o-u-s*, *w-o-m-e-n*, *z-a-m-e-n*. What do these words mean? Since I asked the question in English, the reply, in English, would be "nothing" in the first case, with *nous*, and "nothing" in the third case, *Zamen*. In the second case, *women*, one would answer that in English this is the noun that designates the plural form for females, pronounced—despite orthography—"wimen," not "wohmen" or "wahmen." As for the other words, if we knew Greek, we might remember that *nous*, pronounced "noos," refers to "mind" or "reason." *Zamen* in English yields nothing.

I focus on these words to emphasize the implicit ground of meaning that underlies each first-person-plural reference, for each of these locutions is a reference to the first-person plural: the first from French, the second and third from Chinese. Translinguistic associations are as fascinating and as underrecognized as bilingual puns:[1] one speculates that the intersection of *nous* ("noo") meaning "we" in French and *nous* ("noos") meaning "mind" in Greek may have been fruitful in Cartesian philosophers conversant with Greek. The two Chinese first-person-plu-

---

1. I am reminded of the American tourist in Budapest—who spoke neither Hungarian nor German—who visited the famous baths in that city that date from the Ottoman Empire. To avoid the application of oils to her body, she instructed the attendants, "Dry massage," whereupon she was given three *(drei)* massages.

ral references are useful in illustrating an aspect of "we" references that may not always be obvious—that first-person-plural references are sometimes not equivalent, even in the same language. For example, the Chinese *women*—pronounced "wohmen" but orthographically identical with English *women*—refers generically to any group subsuming the speaker or writer. (A "feminist" clothing store in New York called itself "W-O-M-E-N"— meaning, bilingually, in Chinese and in English, "We, women.")

However, the word *zamen* in Chinese immediately identifies the speaker as coming from north China, specifically from the city of Beijing, and it embodies a subtle modification of the inclusive first-person-plural reference: *zamen* refers, not to any abstract group that includes the speaker or writer, or even to those who are present, but only to those who are actually attending to the speaker. How useful this delimited first-person-plural reference may be will be obvious to anyone who wants to define a group within a crowd—say, a cocktail party—identified solely by a responsiveness to the sound of one's own voice. In other words, anyone who hears this message is part of the "we" reference; anyone, even if physically present, who does not hear or does not attend to the message is not part of the "we" reference. This discrimination of first-person pluralities, between those who are "attending" and those who are not, serves to highlight the implicit ambiguities in the "we" pronoun; it will also serve to underscore the diversities in *us*.

We may ask, Of what (or whom) is the pronoun *we* a sign? In addition to the editorial and the imperial "we's," are there other varieties of "we"? And are there unsuspected problematics in the use of this sign that generally escape notice? Are there implicit as well as explicit "we's"? And can a careful analysis of different uses of *we* reflect some light on ourselves and on our pluralities of self?

Let me begin with a personal anecdote. As a young man, I

worked in a publishing house securing reprint rights for the prestigious Anchor Books line. One of the books in which I was interested was published by the Oxford University Press, which— at the time—denigrated paperback publication and was loath to release their titles for reprint. When I was asked to recommend books that we might publish in Anchor, I mentioned this title. My superior asked, "Who published it?" "Oxford University Press," I said. His reply was hard to forget: with a resigned sigh, he said, "We don't have a Chinaman's chance." I agreed with him, somewhat flushed and self-conscious at my Chinese descent, and hoping he wouldn't notice that he was talking about *my* chances. It was for me the first instance in what I came to characterize as the uses and abuses of the pronoun *we*. Since then, the same notion has been embodied in a joke that has circulated about the Lone Ranger and Tonto. Surrounded by hostile Indians, the Lone Ranger turns to Tonto and says, "Tonto, we are in trouble." To which Tonto replies, "What do you mean *we*, white man?"

It is the white male's meaning of *we*, of course, that has been the target of feminist and black critiques of the dominant ideology, implicit or explicit, reflected significantly in the first words of the U.S. Constitution: "We the people." "We the people" did not include black males, who were not granted the right to vote until 1868, when the Fourteenth Amendment was ratified; nor did "we the people" include women, who did not win the right to vote until 1920, when the Nineteenth Amendment was ratified.

But there are other instances of the co-optive *we*, in which disparate voices are subsumed and erased in a homogenized collective. Having grown up in the United States, I am as susceptible as anyone else to the charms of Cole Porter, one of whose most memorable songs is "Let's Do It, Let's Fall in Love." Imagine my chagrin when, in reading the lyrics of this song in *The Complete Lyrics of Cole Porter*, as published originally in 1928,

I discovered that the first refrain began (instead of the now famous "Birds do it, bees do it") "Chinks do it, Japs do it." Fortunately, Porter changed these lines when he thought that they might prove offensive. But what surprises me, even in retrospect, is that for certain mentalities—including one as sophisticated and educated as Cole Porter, who was, after all, a Yaleman—Chinks and Japs were as far from the human experience as the birds and the bees. The implied "we" or "us" in Cole Porter's song was a sign that designated *American* but it was a notion of *American* that did not include some Americans.

It would be easy to dismiss these concerns as an overpreoccupation with the waywardness of the past: they didn't know any better in those days, we might be tempted to say, implying thereby that the problem is solved and that we, today, do know better. But, alas, there are virulent signs that this anglicization of the oriental, this occidentalizing of the East, this homogenization of the heterogenous, is occurring today in these United States.

One example of the subsumed, homogenous "we" is the rampant and unabashed anti-Japanese sentiment that seems pervasive today. When the Japanese bought Rockefeller Center, it offended the sensibilities of Andy Rooney, the wag of "Sixty Minutes," the socially conscious activist television news magazine.[2] Deftly, but disingenuously, Rooney relates some vicious ethnic jokes, hypocritically distancing himself from them: "The day it was announced that the Japanese had bought Rockefeller Center for $846 million in cash, the joke around the office was, 'Did you hear about Lockefella Centa?'" With scarcely disguised lack of irony, Rooney concludes: "I don't like Japanese real estate giants buying our country. I don't defend it on intellectual grounds.

2. This was written before the more recent controversy about Rooney's allegedly racist comments about blacks reported by the *Advocate*. In retrospect, the interesting thing about these two controversies is that the anti-Japanese slur hardly made a ripple but the antiblack slur did.

4

This is just the gut reaction of an All-American boy who was brainwashed during World War II. I know it's wrong, but I can't help myself" (6 November 1989 [Tribune Media Services]).

It is understandable that one might be upset to have fought for one's country only to lose it to the enemy. But what about fighting for one's country only to have one's property stolen by one's own government? This is precisely what happened to Japanese-Americans who fought valiantly in the Second World War while their families were driven off their own property and sent to relocation camps while their property was put up for sale at bargain basement prices. Some of the most prosperous landowners in California today are the beneficiaries of property illegally confiscated by the United States government from its own Japanese-American citizens. The reparations to the Japanese-Americans voted in 1988 by Congress are a pittance of the value of the land lost.

Andy Rooney's indignation over the Japanese purchase of Rockefeller Center does not stem from a zealous nationalism. Japan did not rank first among foreign countries in holdings in the United States until 1993: Great Britain, the Netherlands, and West Germany, by some counts, owned more of this country than Japan. Yet that did not prevent anti-Japanese panic from taking over in the press. One rarely encountered anti-British slurs, or denigrations of "tulip" culture, or "Kraut" jokes; indeed, the purchase of American corporations, real estate, and property by the English or the Dutch or the Germans hardly makes the news at all. There is a scarcely disguised racism in Rooney's reaction, the same racism that was a factor in the confiscation of thousands and thousands of acres of choice California landholdings from Americans of Japanese descent nearly fifty years ago. No holdings were confiscated during that period from Americans of German or Italian descent, although this country was also at war with Germany and Italy. Rooney is upset about the Japanese buying an American landmark like Rockefeller Center; one wishes that he could have been as exercised about the confiscation of the patrimony of Japanese-Americans by the U.S. government. His "gut reaction" engenders anti-Japanese feeling. What "gut reactions" might there be in Japanese-American soldiers who also fought (many even died) for America in World War II? Indeed, the all-Nisei 442d Regimental Combat Team, which fought in Italy, was one of the most decorated in the war. Why, with the hundreds of war movies celebrating the heroism of American soldiers during the Second World War, is there not a single movie depicting the exploits of these Japanese-Americans?

Around the Christmas season, we often make the blithe assumption that all the world is Christian, that all the world is like us. Well, some of us are not Christians and do not consider ourselves heathens. There are among us, Americans all, devout Moslems, Jews, Buddhists—some resolute atheists and doubting agnostics. Some of us celebrate Hanukkah toward the end of December. Yet our greetings presuppose a "we," an "us" that imposes a homogenized image on others, as if any departure from the model were an imposture or somehow socially deviant. These inadvertent "put-downs" pervade even ordinary speech and are not limited to special occasions. I remember hearing a radio interview with Joseph Papp, born Joseph Papirofsky of Polish Jewish parents in Brooklyn, in which he was asked to comment on his long and distinguished career in the theater. The director of Shakespeare-in-the-Park, the founder of the American Place Theater, and one of the major forces in American drama for the last generation was asked the usual fatuous question: "Mr. Papp, when you started out forty years ago, did you ever imagine that you were embarking on a glorious crusade for American theater?" As near as I can recollect, Joseph Papp replied: "First of all, the Crusades were not glorious, and second of all, *crusade* is not a Jewish word."

Our uses of language, overtly or covertly, embody attitudes, imply a certain "we" that may not be as inclusive as we imagine. Not only is it a matter of good manners—that we don't offend other people. It's also a matter of clear thinking—that we understand the import of what we are saying. Anyone who has spoken of "Jewing someone down," or of "finding a nigger in the woodpile," or of "hitting a Chinese home run," is reflecting bigotries, advertently or inadvertently, that need to be extirpated—all the more because they are insidious and infect the thoughts of even well-meaning people. "Chinks and Japs" are not interchangeable with "birds and bees."

New Yorkers are all familiar with the celebration that occurs each year at New Year's Eve when television and radio focus on that magical moment when the ball on the Times Tower descends at the stroke of midnight. Yet, when I grew up in New York, it didn't dawn on me until quite late—and I suspect that some New Yorkers are still ignorant of the fact—that at the very moment that ball magically descends, in twenty three other time zones in the world, the New Year has already passed or has yet to arrive. In all the time that these broadcasts have been made, no one points out that the importance of that precise moment pertains only to those living in the region that follows Eastern Standard Time. Somehow, it takes the edge off things when you are told about a universal moment that applies only to a twenty-fourth of the world. New York may be—as its promoters say—"where it's at," but it is not the world, even if some New Yorkers think so.

There are, to be sure, inclusive "we's" and surrogate "we's," and the implications of these are worth examining. The inclusive "we" may be represented by this flatteringly comprehensive opening of an article by Carl Sagan: "In October 1957, we humans launched a machine into space that could orbit the earth. Now, less than a third of a century later, we have visited the outermost known planet in the Solar System. We have passed beyond the planetary frontiers. We have explored close-up more than 50 worlds" (*Parade*, 26 November 1989). No one can read this without some sense of pride in this marvelous species that has accomplished all these things. I suppose that humans could be criticized for arrogance by all the other species, all the other life forms, if they only had the intelligence to be captious. Sagan inculcates all of us in "man's glorious achievements" (it is significant that *man* is used). But, try as I might, I resist this supererogation of credit: I do not feel that I contributed in any way to these achievements, not even with my tax dollars. Despite my allegiance to the human race, and flattered as I may be that I conceived, planned, and implemented the Voyager probes, this bit of courteous credit sharing is not—for me at least—credible. And, despite my sense of relatedness to all human beings, I cannot imagine that every human being had a part in this triumph: some of us may have even opposed these intrusions into the heavens on religious or other grounds; others might have decided against space exploration in favor of other priorities. The point here is not to censure Sagan for his generosity in sharing the achievements of the space program with all humans; it is to question a co-optive definition of human that not all humans would subscribe to.

There are also intractable "we's": the "we's" that suggest that others don't count, don't in fact exist, or, if they do exist, are somehow inferior. These we-they intractabilities are most familiar in the obdurateness of partisan thinking. Pseudopatriots declaim atavisms not unlike the fanatical, unthinking enthusiasm of sports fans. The "U.S. English" movement is only the most disturbing form of the preemptive and presumptive "we." Its adherents believe that English must be made the official language of the United States regardless of demographics and regardless of the will of the majority. If the population becomes increasingly Latino/Latina—in California and Florida, Latinos/Latinas are already approaching the majority—they must be prevented from imposing their language on the English-speaking minority. But where is it written that the majority rules only when that majority is English speaking? The majority rules, regardless of its ethnic makeup—even, now, in South Africa. Democracy should not be defined as rule by a white, English-speaking majority. The current white majority had better achieve justice for all, if not for the sake of justice, then for the sake of their own future, for in the twenty-first century the white majority will become the white minority. And, if the majority of whites fail to honor their commitments to present-day minorities, they will be oppressed tomorrow when they become the minority.

The national opinion survey on language usage in the United States sent out by the U.S. English movement contains the following question: "Do you favor providing election materials in foreign languages?" This unfairly begs the question and ignores the fact that what is *foreign* to one American may not be foreign to another American. The definition of *foreign* here is implicitly that which is foreign to a monolingual speaker of English (the incipient bias of designating languages other than English as *foreign* is considered in the next chapter). The "we" here excludes all those who are immigrants, naturalized citizens, for whom *English* was the foreign language; the "we" excludes those who may be comfortably bilingual or trilingual, who may be "naturalized" citizens of the United States who came from another country, whose native language was not English. Then, as if to assign to multiplicity of languages all the ills of the world, the form asks: "In order to avoid the political upheavals over language that have torn apart Canada, Belgium, Sri Lanka, India, and other nations, would you favor legislation designating English the official language of the United States?" There are, to be sure, language-based cultural conflicts in Canada, Sri Lanka, and India, but how much upheaval has there been in Belgium, where they speak French and Flemish? Notice that no mention is made of peaceable Switzerland, where they speak French, German, Italian, and Romansh. There is also no mention of Northern Ireland, where the use of the same language among Catholics and Protestants doesn't seem to have reduced the "political upheavals" in that troubled part of the world.

The "U.S. English Only" movement overlooks the rich linguistic heritage in these United States. It overlooks the fact that Virginia very nearly adopted German at one point as its official language; it overlooks the potential advantage of commanding more languages in a global market. Switzerland again comes to mind: it is important to world affairs out of all proportion to the size of its population, or the extent of its natural resources, or the power of its armies. It overlooks the fact that the real secret of the economic miracle in Japan is that the Japanese have been learning a second language—English—in the last twenty years and that they have been learning it very well.

The U.S. English movement locates the true identity of America in an Anglo-English hegemony, but it overlooks the fact that the railroads in this country were built by Chinese, that the cotton plantations were tilled by blacks from Africa, that the French and Germans settled the Midwest, along with the Scandinavians, that the South was, until Thomas Jefferson, a colony of the French, and that the Southwest was Spanish territory until the second half of the nineteenth century. Despite the myths about the Mayflower, the United States is not New England writ large. The greatest irony is that the U.S. English movement should have been spearheaded by a visible immigrant, S. I. Hayakawa, whom some of the descendants of the Mayflower would doubt-less have spurned. Some Asian Americans have become so occi-dentalized that some of them have themselves become advocates of cultural prejudice—in favor of an Anglo-American ideology and against their own cultural roots. The pejorative symbol for these individuals is *banana*—yellow on the outside, white on the inside.

There is a cultural fascism afoot, represented by the likes of Allan Bloom, E. D. Hirsch, and Francis Furuyama, that sees the triumph of the West as the salvation of the world (there are overtones of the Third Reich in the Triumph of the West). They preach a return to the core values of Western civilization and vaunt the virtues of the Judeo-Christian tradition.[3] Even if one could justify a return to feudal thinking in these days of the global village, even if one could somehow sanction the cultural imperialism that preaches the Westernization of the world, one would have difficulty with the monolithic, purist, one might almost say Aryan, version of history that these cultural reaction-aries purvey, for their vision of a straight-line inheritance from Greek civilization through Europe to the modern Western world cannot be sustained by history. Their view is self-serving and carefully selective. They distort history in the same way that the media have distorted Thanksgiving as a tribute to the pilgrims rather than to the Wampanoag Indians who welcomed the pil-grims. The vision of the demagogues of Western civilization does not include the contributions of non-Westerners to the development of civilization. Where would the revival of classical learning be without the great Arab thinkers Avicenna (980–1037)

3. A Jewish colleague points out that the term *Judeo-Christian* is not favored by "identified Jews": "The phrase strikes me as an attempt by members of either group," he writes, "to erase cultural, religious, and sociopolitical differences that first became insignificant (except as stumbling blocks) in assimilationist climates in 19th-century European countries."

and Averroës (1126–89)? Where would the great explorers be without the compass, which was not a Western invention? Where would the spread of learning be without the invention of rag paper and printing, neither of which were perfected in the West. And is it generally known that one of the most foremost writers of Roman comedy, Terence, was black and a slave?

When in his "End of History" Francis Furuyama writes, "For our purposes, it matters very little what strange thoughts occur to people in Albania or Burkina Faso, for we are interested in what one could in some sense call the common ideological heritage of mankind" (1989, 9), he is mouthing arrogant provincialities. Egypt and Algeria are further away from the Eurocentric center of civilization and might be as remote from Furuyama's purposes as Albania or Burkina Faso. Yet upper Egypt produced Plotinus, the greatest neo-Platonic thinker of the early Middle Ages, who in his youth sought out the wisdom of Persian and Indian philosophy after pursuing his studies in Alexandria. And a little town in North Africa with a name more far-fetched than Burkina Faso, the town of Souk-Ahras, on 12 November 354 produced Saint Augustine, one of the greatest Christian philosophers. The "strange" thoughts in upper Egypt, where Plotinus was thought to have been born, and in Souk-Ahras, birthplace of Saint Augustine, managed to transform Western thought. Their origins outside the citadels of Western thought is, of course, forgotten in the hegemonic interpretation of civilization as an exclusively Western invention. For Furuyama's purposes, the thoughts of the Japanese Zen masters or of the Chinese Confucians or neo-Confucians matter little, despite the fact that they have influenced more than half the world, not all of which is uncivilized.

Even inveterate Anglophiles are beginning to see the light. In a tortuous retrospective of T. S. Eliot in the *New Yorker* (20 November 1989) that reveals both admiration for and revulsion against the Anglo-American poet-dramatist, Cynthia Ozick begins to see her blithe and youthful self as somehow mesmerized by the compulsion to be aristocratically English. Her characterization of Eliot demythologizes him and at the same time reflects a certain self-recrimination: "It may be embarrassing for us now to look back at that nearly universal obeisance to an autocratic, inhibited, depressed, rather narrow-minded, and considerably bigoted fake Englishman—especially if we are old enough (as I surely am) to have been part of the wave of adoration. In his person, if not in his poetry, Eliot was, after all, false coinage" (p. 121). Those who deny their heritage, even if they achieve eminence, are not worth a plug nickel: their species is specious. For Ozick, a Jew, Eliot's anti-Semitism is a bitter pill to swallow. She winces at such excerpts from Eliot as "The rats are underneath the piles. / The jew is underneath the lot" and "Rachel *née* Rabinovitch / Tears at the grapes with murderous paws." Ozick realizes that Eliot's "we" does not include her; in order for her to relate fully to his words, she must betray her Semitic self.

But, for every Ozick who has removed the scales of another's prejudice from her eyes, there are many who are still unaware of the self-deprecations involved in espousing the Western doxology. Furuyama uses the phrase "universal homogenous state" several times, without apparent self-irony: one thinks of the all-American fondness for homogenized white milk, which is offered as a universal panacea, for building healthy bodies and wholesome minds. This vision of homogenized culture has no room for anyone—like some Asians and Jews—who may suffer from "lactose intolerance." But Furuyama's vision is jejune: "In the universal homogenous state, all prior contradictions are resolved and all human needs are satisfied" (1989, 5). He relegates the major human problems to a parenthetical aside: "While there was considerable work to be done after 1806—-abolishing slavery and the slave trade, extending the franchise to workers, women, blacks, and other racial minorities, etc.—the basic *principles* of the liberal democratic state could not be improved upon." The onslaught of a white, Western, Eurocentric hegemonic ideology, in this age, is breathtaking: there is a heedlessness in these sweeping formulations. The irony is that they are made by an American whose skin is yellow and who is himself descended from the Japanese. Furuyama is an exponent of what he is striving for: a universal homogenous state, where everyone in the world will look alike and think alike and the reigning thought pattern would be Western, liberal, and democratic. Orwell presented no prospect more horrific.

But, if certain intellectuals are retreating into feudal and racist thinking, there are signs that the populus is not convinced about a monocultural hegemony in the future. North Carolina, Louisiana, and, most recently, Arizona have all passed legislation that will mandate a second language in elementary school before the year 2000. We will not be distracted by the bilingual debate: the issue should not be whether instruction is offered in either Spanish or English. The issue should be that no American in the future will be limited to one language, whatever that language is. One trusts that at least one of those languages will be English since English is the second language of choice in the rest of the world. The United States must be competitive in its command over second and third languages. There must be a "second language" movement that will ensure that no American will emerge from his or her schooling with fewer than two languages.

The external pressures for this need no repeating, but the internal mandate is not as often recognized. We must promote the *multilingual* speaker of English, not the *monolingual* English-speaking American. We must recapture the multilingual heritage of our own country. This country was not developed by people who spoke English only. Our textbooks have taken note—perhaps because they are in English—of only the records that exist in English. It is ironic that those who favor English only overlook the fact that English is one of the richest languages in the world precisely because it has absorbed influences from the rest of the world's other languages. The advocates of English insist only on linguistic homogeneity, scarcely recognizing that it is heterogeneity that is the strength of the English language. The need to teach a second language in this country is, therefore, not merely a response to external pressures; it stems from an obligation to rediscover our own multilingual past, which, ironically, the early immigrants as well as some more recent immigrants like Hayakawa and Furuyama have assiduously denied.

We must henceforth be distrustful of any unambiguous "we's." As one establishes the European Community, perhaps one should think of Otto van Habsburg, who was in 1989 the seventy-seven-year-old son of Charles IV, the last monarch of the Austro-Hungarian empire. He held Hungarian, Austrian, and West German citizenship and spoke Hungarian, German, English, and French. His example reminds us that the past was neither monolingual nor monocultural; nor will the future be monolingual or monocultural. We have been misled into believing the myth of monolingualism and the false concept of a "universal homogenous state." We have been deluded into thinking that unity depends on uniformity. But our strengths come from diversity, and we should be skeptical of the single-valued "we."

"We, the people" in the United States are many and many splendored: we have been the crossroads of cultures for all the exiles and idealists in the world, for the despised and the enterprising. The Statue of Liberty does not say, "Give me your tired, your poor—provided you promise to learn English"! We will, henceforth, be skeptical of the locution *we*. For in the editorial *we*, the co-optive *we*, the royal *we*, the exclusive *we*, the monolingual *we*, there are wholesale changes of scene, decisive paradigm shifts, that crucially alter the nature of discourse. These locutions may stretch our concept of collective self: perhaps they will remind us of the pluralities in the first-person plural.

CHAPTER TWO

Taking the "Foreign" Out of Foreign-Language Teaching

One of the stumbling blocks to a diverse America is the assumption that all Americans speak English and that one is less American if one speaks another language. This notion of an American as monolingual was exposed by Paul Simon of Illinois, who was at the time a representative to Congress, in a book called *The Tongue-tied American*, published in 1980. Europeans often jibe at Americans with the following anecdote: "What do you call someone who speaks three languages?" "Trilingual." "What do you call someone who speaks two languages?" "Bilingual." "What do you call someone who speaks only one language?" "American."

Yet "foreign languages" have been taught in this country for generations, evidently to little effect. What are the reasons for the persistent monolingualism of Americans, who insist on restricting themselves to English, despite the multilingualism that prevails in the world, even despite the multilingualism that exists in the United States? Why has foreign language instruction effectively failed to produce a multilingual America?

I begin with the following questions. What is being taught in foreign language instruction? Is the study of foreign languages an intellectual discipline, like mathematics or physics, a body of cognitive knowledge, like history or literature, or a technical skill that requires practical training, like surgery? Intellectual discipline, cognitive knowledge, and technical skill—which of these three is primary in foreign language instruction? What are we teaching when we teach a foreign language? What kind of students do we want to produce—someone who thinks deeply, someone who knows a lot, or someone who speaks the language?

Advocates of proficiency would emphatically choose the last option, but, unlike, say, typing or bicycle riding, learning a language is a highly contextual and structured skill: there is an intellectual dimension in the study of the language, implicit in at least the grammar; and, if language is part of culture, it is not possible to acquire a language without absorbing knowledge about the culture it inhabits. Still, it is probably reasonable to expect that, whatever students of French study, they should at least be able to speak French to the French. In that case, then, teaching a foreign language may be more a process of training in a complex of skills than a challenge to the intellect or the transmission of a body of material. We are saying, in effect, that we can accept a student of French who may be ignorant of phonological analysis and of the Carolingian kings (as some Frenchmen and Frenchwomen are), but we cannot accept a student of French who cannot speak and understand French. Indeed, one could put it in the converse: an intellectual knowledge of the phonemic and morphemic structure may positively impede the production of fluent French in a student speaker. One should not forget that there are uneducated people all over the world who are natively fluent.

The products of foreign language instruction in this country have not always met this basic test of functional fluency. Indeed, I venture to say that those who do pass this test are in the distinct minority. Some estimates indicate that "only 17 percent of those who study a foreign language wholly within the United States can speak, write, or read the language with ease" (Simon 1980, 5). If foreign language instruction has produced such indifferent results with respect to its primary mission, if the language has not been taught, then one might ask, What *has* been taught? I contend that, in most instances, what has been taught in foreign language instruction is more the "foreign" than the language.

Let us briefly review the history of foreign language teaching in this country. Unlike the experience in other countries, say, in Japan or Russia or China, the first teachers of foreign languages in this country were predominantly if not exclusively natives in the foreign culture, immigrants from that culture: they were chosen with one qualification, that they were natively proficient in the language. They were undoubtedly qualified *speakers* of the language, but no one thought to ask if they were qualified *teachers* of the language. Indeed, the availability in the United States of so many foreign nationals, not to mention a diversity of ethnic populations who were native in a host of foreign languages, made this process and these assumptions not only natural but inevitable. These instructors had several advantages: they had indisputable authority (although language ability varies even among natives); they were natively expert in their subject matter; and they were natural exemplars of the language they taught. There was one experience, however, that these native teachers of foreign languages lacked: they had never learned the language *as* a foreigner. These native foreign language teachers combined, anomalously, a signal strength with an unnoticed weakness. They knew their subject like the palm of their hand, yet, by that very fact, they were inexperienced about communicating that subject to someone for whom it was not native. (That so many native teachers of foreign languages have developed into effective teachers *despite* these obstacles is a tribute to their resourcefulness and their intuitive brilliance.)

Native teachers of a foreign language were exponents of a culture that, for one reason or another, students found attractive, even exotic. But it would be ingenuous to believe that the motivation of students in learning a foreign language has always been pragmatic, the way a decision to learn PASCAL or FORTRAN or LISP is pragmatic. The choice of a particular foreign language has not been dictated entirely by functional considerations: elements of personal taste and temperament inevitably enter into the picture. Since most native teachers of foreign languages tended to be chauvinistic about their own culture and were untrained in the objectives of second language learning, they naturally relied on mimicry as the most readily available technique of instruction. They invited students to copy them, to be replicas of themselves.

But this simple strategy had two crucial flaws, one methodological, one phenomenological. While it is true that as infants we learn our native tongue by imitation, learning by imitation does not come quite so naturally for adolescents or adults. Nor is the experience of infants learning from their own family equivalent to that of students learning a foreign language: the former are learning language, but the latter already have language and are learning how to be foreign. In the first case, a person is establishing his or her own identity; in the second case, one develops another identity, not to replace, but to supplement the first.

The difficulties of learning a foreign language, it is safe to say, are psychological more than they are logical. Clearly, it doesn't make sense that an intelligent adult has more difficulty learning a language than an infant, yet everyone acknowledges that fact. It doesn't make sense, of course, unless one recognizes that different things are being learned. The infant is acquiring what is to become familiar, even natively familiar; the adult is superimposing the strange onto the familiar. Students of a foreign language imitating a native instructor embody a false phenomenological strategy, one that overlooks an unavoidable existential fact: they can never *be* natives of the foreign culture. Until they have actually lived in the native culture, the best they can hope for, in their minds, is some degree of parody. And what emerges is often not authentic impersonation but a poor imitation.

The student realizes, subconsciously, that there is an imposture going on, just as children balk when asked by parents to "perform" before doting guests, even though they have no difficulty playing "pretend" by themselves. That is why the most effective learners of a foreign language embody the actor's disposition: they are willing to assume any role, to subjugate their own identities, forget their native culture, not so much to speak as to *enact* a foreign language. The subtle difference might be seen in a fine discrimination between "speaking *like* a native" and "speaking *as* a native." The presumptuousness of a nonnative speaker speaking as a native reflects a condescension, an attitude that (here our words betray us) we "have mastered" the language.

Leaving aside the question of what this mastery is or how problematic it is to assume that all natives actually "master" their own language, we may ask if this concept of "mastery" learning is all that appropriate for language learning. Can one "master" French the way one masters typing? We examine students of foreign languages to see if they have achieved "mastery," yet no one has determined what mastery, even for a native, actually consists of. There is also a psychological drawback in this concept *mastery*: it suggests a level of achievement that needs no further development, a static notion of competence. It raises false expectations in the neophyte learner, who asks meaninglessly, Can I really learn Chinese (or Arabic or Russian) in such-and-such a period? What everyone generally has in mind is learning enough to sustain a useful and relevant dialogue in the foreign language, to survive in a foreign culture without recourse to the use of one's native language. Strictly speaking, language cannot be regarded as cognitive subject matter, as if that language were a body of knowledge to be transferred from one brain to another. It is a mode of thinking, an approach to expression, with similarities from language to language, but with many more dissimilarities. Learning a new language is learning a new way of thinking. Too often, foreign languages have been taught as content, as commodities, as so many items of information to absorb. The formulation *teaching Chinese* (or Arabic or Russian) in ordinary language misconstrues the process and misses the objective. What we should be teaching is not the language but rather how the language might be negotiated: we should teach students *how* to learn a specific language as well as *how* to learn *in* that language. These survival skills may be difficult to achieve, and, even when achieved, they fall far short of anything that might be characterized as *mastery*, but they provide the foundation for developing authentic, if not native, users of that language, effective negotiants of that culture. Our "products" in foreign language instruction ought to be students who will, in more that one sense, *act* in that language.

There are books that counsel the student on how to learn a foreign language, in which every other word of wisdom reminds the student that "learning languages is fun." The author's notion of *fun* is never fully defined, but most of what comes across is an adolescent delight in "tricks" and in poses, a complacency about "shortcuts" to learning other languages. While I do not want to denigrate the achievements of polymaths in learning dozens of languages, I do want to question the propriety—psychological, cultural, emotional, perhaps even ethical—of the idea of "picking up" another language. Linguists of this stripe do not see the acquisition of language as a lifetime process of self-discovery in a unique culture; they are marketers in the international bazaar of cultural knickknacks—picked up, if not for a song, then for the price of a phrase book or a grammar. They do not conceive that there may be good reasons for the sometimes intractable difficulties in learning a foreign language and that the difficulties are not merely a restricted phonetic palette, or unfamiliar sounds, or a vagrant grammar. To regard one person's culture as someone else's recreation overlooks the "emic" nature of language; achievement in language fluency must be *earned* as well as learned.

The student of a second language is not psychologically primed to depart from the native language, except for often rather specious motives. There are the *exotica-mongers*, those who, bored with their own ordinariness, acquire a patina of *différance;* there are the *esoterica-mongers*, those who seek out the arcana of a remote subject in a remote language and who value the subject in proportion to its inaccessibility to the general population; and, perhaps most obnoxious of all, there are the *erotica-mongers*, those whose interest in a foreign language is prurient and pornographic and who focus on what might be regarded in their own culture as bizarre and vulgar. Each of these attitudes emphasizes the "foreignness" of the second language. Each of these estranges the student more than it makes familiar. Each of these defines the enterprise of learning a foreign language in terms of what the language is not rather than in terms of what it is.

These motivations, ethnocentric as they may be, may be useful nonetheless to promoting the study of another language, which is extremely arduous, where the results are not immediate, and where the rewards are not always obvious. The peril is in not outgrowing these "liminal" inducements and failing to recognize that no culture is either exotic or esoteric to itself. The study of another culture does not merely offer another perspective; it is often the discovery of a new insights, not only of the other, but also of the self. Any citizen of the world can attest to the old saw that, in order to fully appreciate where one comes from, there is no more effective means than to travel abroad.

In the United States, an untapped resource of motivation is the general need to rediscover one's roots. It is time to overcome the national inferiority complex about language, a complex that is the legacy of earlier immigrant generations who submerged their native language in order to become more quickly acculturated in this country, to become American more quickly (see Sagarin and Kelly 1985; Glazer and Moynihan 1963; and Fishman 1966). That is perhaps the worst consequence of the WASP myth of the all-American perpetrated in this country, to which the English-only movement is a throwback. Americans, especially immigrants, were taught to believe that, to be American, one had to speak English and to speak it without an accent, as if this country were exclusively English in its makeup. This cultural prejudice was symbolized by the not so benign image of the melting pot, where ethnic constituencies would be eliminated in a hodgepodge of bland Anglo-Saxon, Mayflower pabulum. The myth hides an ambivalent truth: that this country, which sees its linguistic identity monolingually, was also built by people who were native speakers of Italian, French, Chinese, Spanish, Japanese, and German. I find it interesting that, in the proliferation of interest in postcolonial cultures, few examine the United States as the *premier* example of postcolonial development: it is as if we were ashamed that we had affinities with the Third World, that we were more like "them" (Africans, Asians, etc.) than like "us" (Anglos, Europeans). No one, to my knowledge, considers American literature "postcolonial literature," even though it was in its earliest stages "colonial."

The predominance of English and of white Anglo-Saxon Protestant culture in defining the American character may be, in the future, a thing of the past. Demographers tell us that, in the decades to come, the Latino/Latina population in this country may be in the majority. That means that, unless we adopt the white minority rule policy, which even South Africa has renounced, we will have to face the prospect of Spanish being the majority native language and English becoming a second language. Some will see this as a threat, but they are responding only to instincts of prejudice and provinciality. The putative monolingualism in the United States is a myth of history, perpetrated by the imperialism of the English language, the result of the United States establishing its identity during the nineteenth century, when English logocentrism in the world was at its height.

The notion of *a* native language, of there being only one native language, is also a chimera. There are many people in the world who are, if not native in more than one language, near native in several. The example of Switzerland comes readily to mind, but one should not overlook the countries of southeast Asia. In Singapore, for example, the national language is English, but the Chinese and Indian populations often speak their native tongues (Chinese, Hindi) at home. The notion of *native* in *native language* is far more problematic in many parts of the world than is recognized (see Coulmas 1981; Paikeday 1985). The Irish would prefer to claim Gaelic as their native language, although most if not all of the Irish speak English. In India, there are *fifteen* official languages, but only English is used as the national language: that means that Indians are variously "native" in Bengali, Tamil, and Hindi as well as in English. In many parts of the world, English is not so much a foreign language as merely another language, whether a second language or the first of several. Of course, the modification of the term *foreign language* into the notion of a *second language* is a helpful neutralization of subliminally incendiary nuances. There are those viscerally adamant provincials for whom *furrin* is a dirty word, a term of abuse, not very different from *barbarian*.

As someone whose face is conspicuously foreign but who has been hopelessly (and, on the whole, happily) Americanized by over forty years in this country, I have had the deliciously ambivalent pleasure of teaching English composition to American students. There are times, I confess, that I see myself as a foreigner teaching American students English *as a foreign language*. Let me share an anecdote that illustrates the differences between conspicuous and nonconspicuous foreigners. Many of my faculty colleagues would be considered ethnically European and labeled by the Immigration and Naturalization Service as *foreign nationals* or *naturalized citizens*. At one party, a faculty member of German descent was speaking in English to a relative of another faculty member who was visiting from Germany. After some minutes, the conversation prompted the faculty member to think of a German proverb, which he first paraphrased in English, then quoted in German, preceding both with the prefatory remark, "In my language, there is a saying. . . ." After hearing the proverb quoted in German, the German interlocutor responded in English with surprised delight: "Why, that's my language, too!"

The concept *foreign* should no longer have currency, least of all in the United States. It is not pedagogically useful, it is not historically accurate, and it is not psychologically valid. When it comes to virtually any "foreign" language, American citizens can be found who would say, "Why, that's my language, too!"

In the last few decades, we have become more and more aware of the inherent tendency of language to influence our thinking subliminally; we have uncovered the heretofore unnoticed ideological bias in English toward the male, toward the white race, and toward Western culture. The phrase "we, the people" has not included all the people: it has promised more than it delivered. There are people—from the black slaves whom Thomas Jefferson owned, to the Chinese coolies who were dynamited along with the mountains to clear the way for the transcontinental railroad they helped build, to the American citizens of Japanese descent incarcerated in Manzanar during the Second World War, to the American Indians who were relegated by

President Reagan to "preservations" at the Moscow summit in June 1988, to the women whose contributions to history and culture have been blithely ignored by generations of male historians—there are people whose experiences belie the democratic ideal that politicians invoke with such glibness. These are the people who have been shortchanged by "we, the people." For the "people" in this country include blacks, women, Italians, Latinos/Latinas, Japanese, Chinese, Arabs, Koreans, and, yes, Vietnamese "fresh off the boat."

The ancestral languages of "we, the people" are Bantu and Mandingo, Italian and Spanish, Japanese and Chinese, Arabic and Korean, Vietnamese and Thai. These are also the languages of "we, the people." And so, for these people, to suggest that any language but English is "foreign" is to deny their linguistic patrimony, to denigrate their origins, to erase their ethnic identity. About these ethnic groups, Joshua Fishman commented more than twenty years ago, "It would seem that as long as these languages and cultures are truly 'foreign' our schools are comfortable with them. But as soon as they are found in our own backyards, the schools deny them" (1966, 387). The Anglo-American myth has prevailed too long. Minority populations collectively made this country; immigrants settled this country. Nothing could be more "un-American" than to deny the cultural pluralism at the heart of this nation.

When we have difficulty competing on the international scene, it is not because we lack a sense of purpose, or a national will, or human resources, but rather because we, as Americans, have forgotten our heritage, the source of our strength. We are all foreigners here; except for the Native American (perhaps), we are all, whether we remember it or not, strangers in a land not our own, but that we have made our own. We have forgotten that what made this country was a rainbow coalition that had already developed long before Jesse Jackson exploited it. If this

27

is a country, more than any other, where dreams have come true, it is because not all those dreams were dreamed in English. Even Hollywood, the dream factory, and now the symbol of America, was built by individuals whose native language was not English: "Russian-Jewish immigrants came from the *shtetls* and ghettos out to Hollywood. . . . In this magical place that had no relationship to any reality they have ever seen before in their lives, or that anyone else had ever seen, they decided to create their idea of an eastern aristocracy. . . . The American Dream—is a Jewish invention" (Jill Robinson, quoted in Terkel 1980, 58; Gabler 1988, 1). Neal Gabler (1988) points out that the founder of Paramount Pictures, Adolph Zukor, was born in Hungary; that Carl Laemmle, the founder of Universal Pictures, was born in Germany; that Louis B. Mayer, head of MGM, was born in Russia; that Benjamin Warner, the patriarch of the Warner brothers, was born in Poland. The Hollywood dream factory was dreamed in Hungarian, in Russian, in Polish—and, probably, in Yiddish.[1] This country was built by Gentile *and* Jew, by whites *and* blacks, by men *and* women.

The United States of America has the unique opportunity to surpass every civilization in history, for no civilization—not the Greeks of the Hellenic period, not the Turks of the Ottoman Empire, not the Chinese of the Tang, not the Romans of Augustus, not the Christians of the Holy Roman Empire—can claim an identity as linguistically and culturally diverse. America can realize the fondest ideal of the medieval humanist who characterized the truly civilized person with this quote from Terence's *Heauton Timoroumenos* (The self-tormentor): "Nihil humanum ab eo alienum est" (Nothing human is alien to him). In its ethnic

---

1. At the American Film Institute tribute to Kirk Douglas, televised on 22 May 1991, Karl Malden remarked, "Only in America. Here I am, Malden Sekulovich, talking to Issachar Danielovitch [Kirk Douglas], while the country looks on."

diversity, the United States of America holds the riches of the world. It should be—but alas it is not—the most linguistically diverse and most multilingual country in the world (see Ferguson and Heath 1981).

Consider the following anomalies in America: a Latino or Latina who goes to a "foreign language" department to learn Spanish; a Chinese American who seeks out an East Asian department to learn Chinese; a Jewish American who does not find Hebrew offered, except perhaps as an adjunct of biblical studies, in a university that purports to represent all knowledge.

I should like to speculate on the future of language teaching and propose a few changes. Institutional inertia will, no doubt, preclude what I propose. Yet I venture these quixotic speculations, not as programmatic recommendations, but as pricks of conscience, a reminder that things as they are may not be things as they should be.

It has been noticed that, while there are departments of French language and literature, departments of Germanic languages and cultures, there are no departments of Arabic science or of Turkish music. The word *culture* may purport to include everything in the language, but one looks in vain in these departments for French mathematics or Chinese physics. Is the "area studies" paradigm for determining academic divisions as appropriate in our configuration of knowledge as it is for our sense of geography? With the proliferation of "area studies" in American universities after the Second World War, the world is divided into distinct areas (East Asia, South Asia, Western Europe, Eastern Europe, etc.), with faculty representing various disciplines (political science, linguistics, literature, economics, history, etc.). The salutary effect of this configuration can hardly be questioned: a geographic region is viewed from as many perspectives as possible and is approached from the vantage points of several disciplines. But the model has its flaws: the "expertise" of certain "area studies" scholars does not always include, for example, proficiency in the language or the languages of the country being studied.

In many cases, we have spawned pseudoexperts who, on the one hand, delve into subjects too esoteric for ordinary citizens to challenge and who, on the other, do not—often cannot—communicate with the natives of the area under study. While there have been signal successes in this typically American "slicing up" of reality known as area studies, there have been more than a few "ugly Americans" who have made a profession (if not a fortune) exploiting the twilight zone between "expertise" and knowledge. If evidence be needed, one might cite the general bankruptcy of American foreign policy in the last thirty years, despite massive infusions, first of the Ford Foundation, and later of federal monies. We have spawned an enclave of experts who remind me of Ernie Kovacs's parody of the old radio show, "The Answer Man," in which experts provided answers to questions submitted by listeners. These answers often began impressively, and pedantically, with the phrase, "That's a common misconception. . . ." Kovacs's parody went like this: "A lady submits this question: 'If the earth is round, then why don't the people in the Southern Hemisphere fall off?' Well, now, ma'am, that's a common misconception. Actually, they are falling off all the time!" It strikes me that some of our area studies experts have been telling us that people in other parts of the globe have been "falling off all the time"!

If this seems far-fetched, consider the key "experts" on the Iranian overthrow of the Shah: the *New Republic* (31 March 1979, 13) reported, "It turns out that only six of the sixty U.S. Foreign Service officers in Iran during the revolutionary year 1978 were minimally proficient in Farsi. . . . The political section contained no one who was fluent in the language for much of the year" (quoted in Simon 1980, 54). Or consider the expertise of

Arabicists. "It has been said," Bernard Lewis writes, "that the history of the Arabs has been written in the West chiefly by historians who know no Arabic" (1973, 22). Or contemplate the following "expert" testimony on Chinese literature, as recently as 1940, in the *New Standard Encyclopedia:* "The Chinese language is monosyllabic and uninflectional. . . . With a language so incapable of variation, a literature cannot be produced which possesses the qualities we look for and admire in literary works. Elegance, variety, beauty of imagery—these must be lacking. A monotonous and wearisome language must give rise to a forced and formal literature lacking in originality and interesting in its subject matter only" (quoted in Brown 1980, 127). The mapping of knowledge in geographic regions is topographically traceable but intellectually suspect. Unlike other academic subjects, area studies is not a single discipline but a conglomeration of different disciplines focused on one area. As an interdisciplinary enterprise, particularly if firmly based on knowledge of the language, area studies can produce new insights, new and more powerful paradigms of understanding. But, when it becomes a congeries of marginal intellects selling intellectual trinkets in an international bazaar, then it hardly deserves serious attention, much less financial support. The strongest area studies programs in the country embody not only breadth of coverage but also deep familiarity with the culture, which includes, of course, proficiency in the languages involved.

One of the prospects of the future is the possibility that departmental lines might follow more rationally valid disciplinary lines. There are true as well as specious boundaries between departments. The discipline of mathematics is clearly different and distinct from the discipline of history, but can one detect a disciplinary difference between a department of French and a department of English? These designations subsume language, literature, as well as *culture* (somewhat limitedly defined) since they implicitly exclude the more scientific and mathematical subjects. If the study of literature is a discipline, then that discipline is the same whether French literature or Chinese literature is being studied. Yet we insist on dividing our departments on the basis of content and from a Eurocentric perspective. There are the European languages, and there are the others—usually known as *non-Western*. When budgets get tight, the first instinct of administrators is to group the "others" together. They might as well be honest and label these conglomerations *etc.*

One might also ask if the very makeup of the departmental structure in the university is very useful when literature teachers and language teachers are lumped together in an uneasy truce. In English departments, teachers of composition are often relegated to the lower echelons, and the professors of literature occupy the upper reaches. In the foreign language departments, those who teach the language are subordinate to those who teach the literature. These generic tensions have not been salutary either for the teaching of literature or for the teaching of language. The inclusion of English and American literature in English departments is a significant instance of composite nationalism: the two literatures are seen as mutually reinforcing. The alliance is promoted in the United States because British English is considered a progenitor of American English; but, in Great Britain, the amalgam is scarcely tolerated, and "American studies" remains a separate—and is considered in many places an inferior—subject.

What would make more sense is if, in the future, three separate departments were established, each with subareas of interest (on the model of, say, chemistry, which subsumes organic, inorganic, quantitative, molecular, physical, and biological chemistry; or physics, which subsumes quantum mechanics, astrophysics, plasma physics, and environmental physics). The logical division for what constitutes the presently constituted foreign language departments would be a department of linguistics, a department of language, and a department of literature. Linguistics already exists as a separate department, but language and literature are still lumped together, and the national distinctions persist, unhelpfully.

The divisions of national literature perpetrate an unbalanced view of history: they promote the notion that the subject is as comprehensive as the other disciplines that range through time and space; they neglect the fact that nationhood is a recent concept and that, in the history of the world, nationalism is only a recent phenomenon. Nationalisms are a legacy of the nineteenth century. They are increasingly untenable in the twentieth century. They have no future in the twenty-first century. The European Community, OPEC, the NICs (newly industrializing countries), the "Little Tigers," the Third World—these are becoming the coalitions of the future. In the global village, the global economy, more and more, nationalisms are becoming anachronisms. International corporations are, in some cases, more powerful than nations; in the world of the future, as Walter Wriston, former CEO of Citicorp, has argued in *The Twilight of Sovereignty* (1992), the nation-state concept doesn't make as much sense as it once did.

One overlooks the fact that, before the First World War, there were no passports, which were devised at first as a temporary measure but which have continued on their own momentum. The passage of NAFTA, the promulgation of GATT, the fall of the Iron Curtain, the joyful destruction of the Berlin Wall—all remind us that many of the barriers impeding concourse between human beings are made by humans and can be removed by humans. Indeed, one could suggest that the die-hard nationalists, explicitly in Ireland, or in South Africa, or in the Middle East, and implicitly in the United States, Japan, the former Soviet Union, and China (both the People's Republic of China and the Republic of China), are the source of most of the conflicts all over the world. The emergence of the separate cultures in the Soviet Union (Latvia, Lithuania, Estonia among them), the demands for sovereignty by the Kurds and Shiites in Iraq, the separatist ambitions of the Sikhs in India—these are not merely throwbacks to the past; they are also harbingers of the future. Nationalisms are pseudocivilized reversions to visceral impulses; jingoisms have not evolved very far from atavisms.

I am far from counseling a reversion to the "melting pot" myth: the global village must retain its ethnic diversity, even while it reduces frictions between nations. There is a difference between *nationalisms*, definition of a group by citizenship and by political fiat, and what I would call *ethnicisms*, definition of a group by a distinct linguistic heritage. Many Quebecois in Canada are motivated by an "ethnicism" that is evidently stronger than their "nationalism." The nationalist agenda promotes an allegiance to a political concept, a polity, in which identity could be conferred or removed only by the state. But "ethnicisms" are a throwback to history and to linguistic origins. "Culturalisms," not nationalisms or ethnicisms, will be the wave of the future. *Culturalisms* I define as congeries of common interest, which may include a common language and a common culture, but which may also comprise a common interest in democracy, in the environment, in science and art. There is, for example, a distinct "computer culture," an "e-mail culture," even a "Dungeons and Dragons" culture. Scientists and artists regularly disregard nationalisms and language barriers and ethnic differences. Nuclear physicists, for example, often have more in common with their colleagues in other countries, or with colleagues who speak what is for them a foreign language, than with their own compatriots. One hears reports of white Americans in Silicon Valley and at the Institute of Advanced Study in Princeton wanting to learn Chinese so that they can get access to what they suspect are the most creative ideas in the field—which, apparently, are being discussed in Chinese. In the 1970s and 1980s, computer science in the United States was overwhelmed by foreign students whose grasp of English was, in most cases, minimal, yet that did not prevent them from succeeding in degree programs and in undertaking productive research. Art, of course, being nonverbal, has always transcended language as well as cultural boundaries. The "fauvism" found in Picasso, Matisse, and others anticipated by at least a generation the popular interest in and fascination with African culture. With the establishment of the information highway and the emergence of such networks as Internet,[2] there are new congeries, new "cultures" being formed that no longer focus on a common geographic origin, or a common historical experience, or a common "natural language." In more than one sense, "artificial intelligences" will vie in the future with "natural intelligences."

My wish to take the *foreign* out of *foreign language instruction* reflects the same irony as a bumper sticker that reads, "Help Stamp Out Foreign Languages—Learn One!" I happen to believe that, while there are differences between first and second language acquisition, from a pedagogical point of view, from an intellectual standpoint, language teachers, whether of English or of non-English languages, have more in common than they recognize. Only ethnocentrism keeps them apart. I believe that the existence of the Association of Departments of English separate from the Association of Departments of Foreign Language is a political statement: the distinction has no intellectual bearing, no real academic justification. Only when we define new configurations along truly disciplinary lines—whether of linguis-

2. In a few short years, Susan Estrada estimates in *Connecting to the Internet* (1993), Internet has attracted over 15–30 million users in 137 countries and is adding a million users a month!

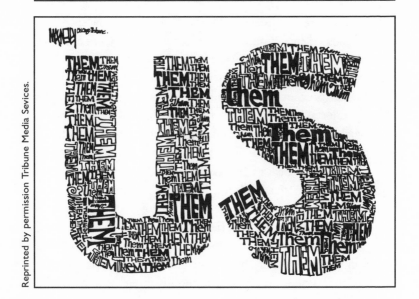

tics, language, or literature—can we escape the evil karma of what I call *negative identities,* those implicit in such locutions as *non-Western, foreign, un-American.* Convenient as these configurations have been in the past, when, in the minds of many, the world was coterminous with the boundaries of one's own country, they are the delusions of the past that need to be dispelled before we can approach the future with any confidence.

CHAPTER THREE

Seeing with Another I:
Our Search for Other Worlds

I n the major intellectual movements in this century, it is now clear—as we approach the end of the century—that a recurrent theme runs throughout the various discoveries and insights in different fields, from relativity theory, to quantum mechanics, to the Heisenberg principle, to phenomenology, to semiotics, to deconstructionism, to chaos theory. Different as these paradigms are, they all highlight the relation between the object and the subject, between the knower and what is known. In each of these mind-sets, the traditional opposition of bipolar thinking is undermined, and a dialectical model of knowledge has been posited. To put it simplistically, We are what we know, and what we know defines who we are. A corollary would be, *How* we know affects *what* we know. Our modes of knowing have become as much a subject for our research as the objects that we strain to discover.

One accessible approach to uncovering what we take for granted—which is one way of saying, to make a discovery—is to examine some of our most familiar reference points. Certainly, the most familiar are the four cardinal directions: north, south, east, and west. One cannot imagine a culture that does not have these basic concepts. Now, while there are commonalities in the etymology of these markers in different languages—in most languages, for example, east is associated with the sun rising and west with the sun setting—still, the four directions assume different valuations in different languages. If, for example, one is asked to name the four directions in order, there are twenty-four possible permutations in the sequence in which they can be named: in English, the two most common are north, south, east, west, or north, east, south, west; English inherits its order from German, where it is north, east, south, west, and from French, where it is north, south, east, west. However, in Chinese, one cites the four cardinal directions is the order east, south, west, north, whereas in Japanese, which uses the same Chinese characters to mark the directions, the order is east, west, south, north. Nor can one assume that the order of citation is totally random. When I asked a German colleague in what order he would cite the four cardinal directions, he said, "Of course, it has to be clockwise: north, east, south, west." That *of course* is not all that obvious. Why, for example, start with north? Not all cultures do. Nor is clockwise so inevitable since "clockwise" need not have been "clockwise" but its opposite if clocks had been invented in the southern rather than the northern hemisphere. The clock replaced the sundial as the preferred means of measuring time (at least in the West: in China the clepsydra, or water clock, was the timepiece of choice, and there was no sense of clockwiseness). In the northern hemisphere, the shadow of the sun moves in what we know to be a "clockwise" direction. However, in the southern hemisphere, the shadow would have moved in the opposite direction (Feldman 1987, 150).

Of the four directions, *north* is privileged in Chinese because it was associated with the emperor, who generically occupied the northernmost residence in the capital and faced *south*. Japan, as the land of the rising sun, seems to have given a special place to *east*. *West*, as a direction, has been associated, at least since the age of exploration in the West, with discovery and adventure, with sailing off into the unknown, with new opportunities and new perspectives. East has been associated with origins, west with destinations: "Go West, young man," Horace Greeley said. While its opposite corollary, "Go East, old man," is not as familiar, the east has often been characterized as the direction toward which one turns for wisdom rather than discovery, for the origin of things, for insight and transcendental knowledge rather than new experiences and new worlds: *ex occidente lex, ex oriente lux* the medieval aphorism went, "out of the west law, out of the east light."

Left-handedness and right-handedness are, as we all know, not neutral concepts. In many cultures, left is considered deviant and unorthodox (vestigial in the etymology of such words as *sinister,* which originally meant "left-handed"). The preponderance of right-handedness among world civilizations has occasioned heightened interest in the brain research of the Russian physiologist A. R. Luria in the 1940s, now familiar in the concept of the so-called bicameral brain. This concern with left- and right-handedness in the universe was highlighted by the discoveries of Tsung-tao Lee and Chen-ning Yang, for which they won the Nobel Prize in 1957. Those discoveries posited parity in the subnuclear universe and left- and right-handedness in the elementary particles in nature. Yet, despite these decisive proofs of left- and right-handedness in the universe, many right-handed people are scarcely aware that right-handedness is a "pseudouniversal."

For example, some arbitrary conventions that seem so familiar are at bottom not arbitrary—the "qwerty" typewriter keyboard, for example, which was presumably based on the frequency of the letters and the relative dexterity of each of the ten fingers. English speakers are often not aware of the fact that the keyboard is different for other—even cognate—languages. Before word processors and electric typewriters, the carriage return lever on manual typewriters was on the *left* side. Indeed, almost all typewriters manufactured after 1910 had left-hand carriage returns. Now, this seems a trivial enough detail, until one stops to think that pulling the carriage return lever with the left hand—in some cases with the left pinky, perhaps the least dexterous of the ten digits—doesn't make very much sense for the 83–90 percent of the population that is right-handed. Indeed, ergonomics would suggest that, instead of requiring operators to use the left pinky at the periphery of vision to pull a heavy carriage and return it to the right does not make as much sense as having the carriage return lever move toward the center, just above the keyboard, where it might be pulled with the strongest digit for most people, the right thumb. Yet, despite these considerations, the preponderant majority of typewriters were manufactured for half a century with a left-hand carriage return.

How did this come about? Well, the company that dominated the office typewriter market in those years, particularly in the early stages, was the Underwood Office Machines Corporation. Underwood's corporate president was, as it turns out, left-handed. So, for more than a generation, millions of right-handers used an instrument that favored a left-hander—one of the few times that left-handedness has been privileged in our society.

You may wonder why no one ever thought of this and considered a carriage return that would be more convenient for right-handers to use. Well, they did. Some of the early typewriters, including one invented for the L. C. Smith company by Carl Gabrielson in 1904, do have a right-hand carriage return, which is much easier for right-handers to use than conventional manual typewriters. At the end of a line, the carriage return lever ends up just above the keyboard, at the center of the typist's field of vision, rather than far out to the periphery of vision at the left; the thumb grasp extends downward so that the right thumb has no difficulty finding it. This configuration is much easier to use for someone who is right-handed.[1]

The point of the anecdote is that, even when they are initially awkward, conventions appear natural and inevitable with repeated use. Our blindness to these biases is reflected in an unfairness to left-handed people, who have to adapt to a right-handed world. Now, even if one recognizes that the preponderant majority of the population is right-handed (estimates range from 80 to 90 percent), that doesn't justify the imposition of right-handed equipment on left-handed people. Anyone who has been left-handed at a crowded dinner table, for example, or who has tried to take notes in classroom seats with the writing surface designed for right-handed people will have some idea of what left-handed people have to put up with in a predominantly, but not comprehensively, right-handed world. Virtually all single doors, for example, favor the right-handed person entering. (Conversely, do the same doors favor the left-handed person exiting; if so, does this say anything about our attitude toward right-handers and toward left-handers?)

Ironically, in some activities, the unconventionality of left-handers is an advantage, as in some sports, like baseball and tennis and, possibly, basketball and boxing. In the 1992 presidential election, all three presidential candidates were left-handed. My point is not that there is a prejudice for or against left-handed people: it's that the right-handed world often doesn't see things from a left-handed (sinister?) point of view. We have raised our consciousness about many human sensibilities, from ethnic minorities to women to "the differently abled," but there appears to be no concerted effort to advance the interests of "the differently handed."

---

1. For the skeptical, I can offer witness since I own such a typewriter and use it regularly (cf. Herrl 1965).

Let me consider another set of directional biases that may not be obvious. In the West, and in this country in particular, forward is favored over backward; what is ahead is favored over what is behind. Implicit in this is a preference for the future, what lies ahead, over the past, what lies behind. We trust what is before our eyes and are made anxious by what is in back of us. We distrust those who work behind our back, and we tend to trust those with whom we see eye to eye. Yet we may be as deceived by what we see as comforted by what we do not see. The most deceptive salesmen have trained themselves to make "eye contact" in order to complete a sale. And those who are truly trustworthy do not need to be monitored and do not need to work before our very eyes.

The bias in favor of forward and against backward may be reflected in the biblical injunction "Get thee behind me, Satan!" which expresses a determination to mend one's ways, to avoid the temptations of sin henceforth. The suggestion is that one yielded to sin in the past but that, in the present and in the future, Satan will have no sway over the faithful. Yet, when this passage was translated into the Quechua language, the translator encountered a difficulty because, in that language, the logic underlying the orientation of past and future to what is in front and what is behind was the reverse of what we are accustomed to. The logic of this Indian tribe went as follows: One knows the past because one has lived it; hence, one can see the past; it is, therefore, before your eyes. Who among us can see clearly into the future? Except for seers and prophets, no one. Hence, the future, being unknown, is not before one's eyes; it cannot be seen and hence can plausibly be assumed to be behind, eternally eluding our view. Hence, the past is in front, before our eyes; the future cannot be seen and is, therefore, behind us. So, in order to preserve the directional biases of each language as well as to capture the original sense of the passage, our "Get thee behind me, Satan!" must be translated in Bolivian Quechua as "Get thee in front of me, Satan!" (Nida 1966, 12).

The reckoning of time and age is another example of a pseudo-universal. A person's age in the West does not correspond to a person's age in China, for example. Time is computed on an absolute scale in the West; a person's age is determined by the exact amount of time he has lived. But, in China, the question about a person's age asks—more literally—in how many calendar years a person has lived, which is not entirely the same thing. Farmers are familiar with calculating how many springs they've lived through: two springs can be as short as a little over a year or as long as more than two years, just short of three. In addition, the Chinese date approximately from conception, not birth, so that, when babies are born, they are one *sui*, a year old. In other words, a baby is a year old in the calendar year in which he is born, even if it's only a month before the end of the year. On New Year's Day, everyone adds a year to his or her age. New Year's Day is, in a sense, everyone's birthday. So, in point of fact, a baby born a month before the New Year can be in his second year by his second month: he is one *sui* at birth, and then a month later, because of New Year's Day, he is two *sui*. If one assumes that there is an inclination to "age" persons faster than one might prefer to be aged in the West—that impression would be, I think, fairly accurate. In China, it is a compliment to be thought older than one really is. There is in Chinese the saying "Zhong lao, qing xiao," which means to prefer age to youth—which seems to be the reverse of what it is in America, where old age is deplored and youth privileged. The forces that one admires here are energy, vitality, dynamism, freshness, daring, innocence—all attributes of youth. Senility, fuddy-duddyness, timorousness, decrepitude—these are all attributes of old age. Yet the obverse is conveniently ignored: thoughtlessness, imma-turity, and self-centeredness (not so attractive tendencies) are also commonly encountered in youth, just as steadfastness, consistency, constancy, loyalty, perseverance, and wisdom are often identified with the old. If we appreciate this point, we can understand why the Chinese appreciate age and deprecate youth.

There is also a telescoping of a generation as a marker of time. In biblical times, a generation meant a thirty-year period, but, in this computer age, a generation has diminished to a third of that. The first electronic computer can be dated to 1939, and we are already into our "fifth generation" and are fast entering the "sixth generation" of computers. Technological generations advance faster than human generations, and they are becoming shorter and shorter. The point is that the use of *generation* in the nonhuman context is by way of analogy to human generation, but the psychological effect of this on humans is hardly negligible. Not many people think of thirty years any more when they think of a generation. The point is that the rapid increase in technological developments, resulting in shorter and shorter periods between "generations," has the net effect of "collapsing" time for us. We live through more significant generations of change in ten years than our ancestors lived through in lifetimes.

Perhaps the most dramatic contrast to be found in conceptual ethnocentricities concerns the notion of the self. American society since Freud has been preoccupied with the self in its various guises. I once checked the number of books in print with the word *self* in the title: there were 4,189, which reflects the pervasiveness of the concept. The stress on the self seems particularly prominent in this country: there is even a periodical out now with the title *Self.* Is it coincidental that English is the only language in the world that superannuates the self punctuationally by capitalizing its first-person-nominative-singular reference: *I*? All other Indo-European languages using the Roman alphabet and Western orthography cite the first-person nominative in lowercase letters: French *je*, German *ich*, Spanish *jo*, Italian *io*.

It is an article of faith—particularly among the young—that a meaningful activity is to search for the self. No one seems to ask whether there is a self to be found. Still, there are certain illogicalities that elude notice: how is it, I'm prone to ask, that, if one hasn't found oneself, one is so sure that the self exists? And, if one is constantly in search of oneself, who or what is doing the searching? Does it make sense for the self to search for itself? Yet inherent in these irrationalities is a cherished premise: that everyone has an individual self, however ill defined, however unformed or wayward, however indeterminate. Our entire liberal, democratic tradition, our belief in freedom and liberty, depends on the reality of this self.

Yet the concept of the individual self, as a separate, privileged entity set apart from the community, is a fairly recent development, even in the West. Its pervasiveness blinds us to other notions of existence that stress the contiguity of humanity rather than the atomistic autonomy of each individual. For anyone who has dealt with adolescent children or teenage students, the supreme expression of the independence of the self, which too often goes unchallenged, is, "It's my life, and I can do anything I want with it!" Yet this blatantly ignores the fact that there are two parents who contributed to our being. If we go back two generations, there are four other human beings involved in who and what we are: going back each generation doubles the number of progenitors. If we assume, as most intelligent humans believe, that we are continuously descended from hundreds if not thousands or millions of generations since the first humanoid emerged, then it isn't hard to imagine that there are whole populations in us, represented by our ancestors and reflected in our genes.

To reverse the issue, and perhaps to satisfy our most egoistic urges, one could cite the thousands and millions of offspring of whom we could be a progenitor. We can be, we may be, fathers and mothers to entire populations! When viewed in this context, it is hard to understand just what it means to say, "It's my life, and I can do anything I want with it!" This claim is based on no factual premise and recognizes no plausible prospect for the future. When one decides, for example, not to have children, not to continue the family line, one is discontinuing a tradition that has existed since the beginning of human civilization, for our very lives are testimony to at least one unbroken line of procreation from generation to generation since the dawn of humanity to the present. Indeed, without this unbroken chain, each of us would not have seen the light of day; none of us would be alive today. We owe our very existence to a continuous line that we threaten to cut off when we decide that we will not have children. At least that's the way Confucians would think. Whether or not one subscribes to that point of view, one must acknowledge that the self may not be as autonomous or as independent as some would like to think.

The present "postmodern" world confronts us with a wealth of paradoxes that emerge from the demands that come from different senses of responsibility. According to the "consanguine-ous" theory of humankind, most conspicuously perpetuated by the Chinese (and specifically Confucian) emphasis on family and the continuity of the family line, it is an impiety not to produce offspring. The traditional need for offspring to worship their ancestors as well as the premodern need for additional "hands" to help with the physical labor in an agricultural society rein-forced the benefits of multiple births. In the twentieth century, however, with its now global interest in individual rights, the recognition of finite resources, and the urgent need to stem the population explosion, multiple births can no longer be as easily justified as they have been in the past. The anomalies created by paradigm shifts run rife. Whereas, in the traditional thinking, multiple births were an obligation to one's family and to society, in the modern and postmodern eras they are thought to be an excessive burden, in view of the strain on the planet's limited resources. In the feudal period, one might consider it selfish not to have many children; in the modern era, on the contrary, having many children may be regarded as a thoughtless self-indulgence. Indeed, one of the urgent needs of our time is to reexamine the notion of self. How narrowly and broadly should one construct this concept? In promoting individual rights for others, are those who enjoy the benefits of individual freedom acting selfishly or unselfishly? Privileging the value of the self over the family and society can be characterized as selfish, but to insist that every individual on the planet should enjoy the same individual rights is anything but selfish.

There are many societies that have no concept of self apart from one's community. For example, according to Godfrey Lienhardt, the Dinka in Africa "have no conception which at all closely corresponds to our popular modern conception of the 'mind,' as mediating and, as it were, storing up experiences of the self" (1961, 149–51; see also Tuan 1982, 142). The Chinese have perhaps the most elaborate reinforcement of this "fact of life" in their family structure. In a traditional premodern Chinese family, each relative has a special name, depending on three factors: whether the relative is male or female, older or younger, and on the mother's or the father's side. In other words, your cousin who is the daughter of your mother's sister and younger than you has a different label, a different term of address, than a cousin who is the daughter of your father's sister and older than you. There are, in fact, names for virtually every possible relative extending over five generations. Each time one refers to a relative, in whatever context, one invokes an entire onomastic network that reminds one of one's place in a multigenerational family. In this welter of relations, it would be hard to conceive of the self as separate. (Is it any wonder that some Western

47

observers have noticed the significance of the fact that, in China, there is no word meaning "privacy"?)

In some of my comparative studies,[2] I have analyzed various contrasts between Western (specifically American) and Eastern (specifically Chinese) ways of conceiving of the world. One of these examples relates to the mind/heart question. In the West, it is axiomatic that the mind thinks and the heart feels. Subject to the test of ordinary language, the obverses of these formulations seem awkward, far-fetched, if not meaningless: "the heart thinks," "the mind feels." In this premise, there are two possibly factitious assumptions: that emotion and mentation are separate or separable and that each can be assigned to either the head or the heart. This dichotomy is so strong that common parlance enshrines the difference, as when, for example, one is warned against "thinking with one's heart" or when one is being asked, rhetorically, "Is that your head or your heart talking?"—as if to suggest that it would be a supererogation of authority for the heart to talk.

These distinctions are left meaningfully vague in Chinese, which regards *xin*[3] as the seat both of emotion and of thought. The very earliest dictum on Chinese poetry—*shi yan zhi*—will be affected by this disjunction between Western and Chinese notions of what might be "psychological physiology," for this phrase can be tenably translated either as "poetry expresses intention"

2. This section derives in part from my "Polar Paradigms in Poetics: Chinese and Western Literary Premises," in *Comparative Literature East and West: Traditions and Trends* (Honolulu: East-West Center, 1989), p. 11–21, which also appears as chapter 13 in my *Transparent Eye: Translation, Chinese Literature, and Comparative Poetics* (Honolulu: University of Hawaii Press, 1993), 238–69.

3. I use the *pinyin* transliteration system here. It is not possible to be totally consistent in transliterating Chinese. Wade-Giles is traditional, but *pinyin* is becoming more and more current. Mao Zedong *(pinyin)* is encountered as often as Mao Tse-tung (Wade-Giles), Tèng Hsiao-p'eng (Wade-Giles) is not as familiar as Deng Xiaoping, and almost no one (outside Taiwan) would use Chao Tzu-yang (Wade-Giles) for Zhao Ziyang *(pinyin)*. Where relevant, I offer the alternative version in parentheses.

(which is its usual rendering) or as "poetry expresses emotions." The word *zhi* is composed of the ideographs *shi* (scholar or soldier) and *xin* (heart-mind). But neither translation of *shi yan zhi* really does justice to the original, for poetry in Chinese can express both thought unalloyed with emotion and emotion devoid of thought. Most commonly, however—and there is in this an implicit value judgment—good poetry expresses a fusion of both feeling and thinking. There is, in Chinese aesthetics as well as in Chinese ethical teaching, a distrust of both pure mentation and pure emotion. In Western terms, the heart is a check on the coldness of the mind, the mind on the fervency of the heart. But this formulation also reflects a bias, for it assumes that two prior entities must somehow be brought together in a symbiosis, when, in the Chinese view, the situation is quite the opposite. The two faculties are not two but one, and it is their separation, either in abstract or in concrete terms, that violates the wholeness of things and creates distortions that disrupt the natural order.[4] We need not pause to consider which view of things is correct: indeed, there are adherents of both points of view, and it may turn out that they are not contradictory.[5]

Two adjustments in premise interpretation are available to resolve the dilemma. First, there might be no division between

4. Two passages in the *Mencius*, fairly close to each other, illustrate the latitude of the word *xin*. Book 2A, chap. 2, verse 1, refers to the "unperturbed mind." When asked whether his mind were perturbed, Mencius replies, "No. At forty, my mind was unperturbed." Yet, several verses later (verse 6), Mencius says, "All men have a mind which cannot bear to see the sufferings of others." Western readers would understand the first "mind" to be the thinking organ and the second "mind" to be the feeling organ, but in Chinese the same word, *xin*, is used in both cases. (I take this translation from Lau [1970].)

5. Recent developments in Western medicine have revived previously discarded notions of mind-body influences, although "holistic medicine" is still greeted with skepticism from the majority of doctors trained in the Western tradition (among the many considerations of this issue, see Goleman [1987] as well as Bill Moyers's PBS television series "Mind and Body").

heart and mind and hence no hierarchy necessary between the faculty of thought and the faculty of feeling: there can, therefore, be no qualitative difference between an assertion of the mind and an assertion of the heart (both would be represented by the word *zhi*, which denotes both intention and conation). In Western law, it is crucial—if difficult—to distinguish between what is intentional and what is unintentional because that distinction will determine the severity of the crime, whether one has committed, say, first- or second-degree murder. Second, there is no real exclusivity in the human capacity for feeling: it doesn't take a rampant animism to entertain the prospect of sentience being variously attributed to all creation.

In the West, the dominance of corresponding abstract-concrete pairs—whether ideal-real, or abstract-concrete, or noumenon-phenomenon—reflects a conception of validation posited on separable categorical worlds, whose very plausibility depends on their being autonomous realms of existence. Conflations of the ideal with the real, the abstract with the concrete, the noumenal with the phenomenal, are difficult, if not impossible, to grasp. In any event, they would erode the clarity, hence the usefulness, of these concepts if their very conceptual purity is sullied. Furthermore, the logic of Western validation, and of Western epistemology, stresses the persuasiveness of correspondence as a factor in truth functions, whether that occurs in Plato's *Republic*, or Augustine's *City of God*, or Dante's *Divine Comedy*. In other words, an abstract system appears more plausible, not because it has been proved logically, but because it resembles something with which one is already familiar. A modern example is the extra suasive power of the observation that the subatomic universe resembles solar systems, with the nucleus corresponding to the sun, the electron to the planets. This analogy may or may not be apt, but we are more likely to credit the theory because of our partiality to correspondence as a mode of "proof." One is more inclined toward accepting validity in the presence of correspondence than in its absence, although no prior proof has been given as to the role of correspondence as a warrant of validity. It may be that correspondence is a heuristic rather than a validating factor, that is, it inspires the human brain with confidence because it is easier to understand (because it reinforces prior knowledge) rather than because it is inherently valid. Departures from correspondence schemes are viewed with suspicion, are seen *as* deviations rather than as data in their own right. The character of knowledge gained by positing a correspondence between an otherworldly and a this-worldly realm is powerfully familiar, of course, with the Platonic vision of the cosmos, where the immutable realm of the Ideas exists concurrently with the mutable realm of diurnal reality. This notion of separateness of the permanent and the impermanent, of the universal and the particular, the perdurable and the ephemeral, pervades much of Western philosophy and poetics.

But these familiar contrasts are not as persuasive in an ontology or epistemology that sees wholeness and change, oneness and immanence, as the warrants of reality. We might posit Chinese forms of validation as those that identify a "resonant immanence." The suasions of Chinese philosophy do not develop out of abstract reasoning, or by a logic of correspondences, but by an appeal to the experiential corroboration of the reader. Consider, for example, the following text from the *Mencius:* "Therefore, what is relished in the mouth is the same in everybody; the sounds perceived by the ear are heard alike by everybody; the colors of the eye are alike, beautiful to all. When one reaches the mind, is it alone without agreement on such things as 'principle' or 'righteousness'? The sages arrive at earlier what my mind already confirms, and therefore 'principle' and 'righteousness' gratify my mind, just as the meats of the table gratify my mouth" (*Ssu-pu pei-yao,* 11:8b; translation mine).

There is more than analogy here, more than correspondence. The argument is, If you can taste, hear, and see, then you must acknowledge the reality of "principle" and "righteousness." The reality of these experiences, their immanence in our experience, compels us to acknowledge the reality of the abstractions proposed: there is no "proof" beyond the heightening of experience, for if each of us can experience "the meats of the table" gratifying our mouths, we cannot then deny the existence of "principle" and "righteousness." The appeal in this discourse is to the immediacy of our own experience, not to an abstract principle beyond our own experience. Note how the citation skips neatly over the deviations of apperception in tasting, hearing, or seeing *(de gustibus non est disputandem);* it seems that verification in the mind of the reader is sought for "principle" and "righteousness," in terms as natural (hence as real) as tasting, hearing, and seeing.

The tendency in some Chinese texts to derive mysteries from actual experience may be contrasted with the Platonic practice of imagining an abstract realm that corresponds to concrete experience or with Aristotle analyzing concrete particulars to discover abstract universals. For a number of significant Chinese philosophers, the division of the abstract and the concrete is untenable: truths derive from the actuality of experience, not in spite of it. There is a resolute insistence that diurnal experience, actuality, is the only reality, and there is an inherent skepticism of that which can be abstracted as being nonexistent. Ancient Chinese philosophical texts, whether Confucian or Taoist, share with Aristotelians, empiricists, and logical positivists the notion that no truth is to be credited that is not grounded on actual experience. Where Chinese philosophy departs from Western notions, however, is in the tendency of ancient Chinese discourse to require an assertion to be felt in human terms, not merely abstractly and intellectually recognized.

An example from Liu Xie's *Wenxin diaolong* illustrates the

point: "Natural excellence may be compared to the splendors of flowers in the woods; their vivid beauty is like the silk-dyed vermilion and green. Silks dyed vermilion and green are deep, rich and vibrant; the blossoms and the sun-drenched trees, blaze forth in glory. Brilliant writing radiates in the garden of literature in much the same way" (Shih 1983, 1). It would be a serious misreading of this text to see Liu Xie (Liu Hsieh) as merely intending a metaphor between "the blossoms of nature" and the "flowers of literature," although the translation easily accommodates such an interpretation. The aptness of the comparison lies in no correspondence between the characteristics of nature and of literature: the force lies in the similarity of experience in one's reaction, on the one hand, to nature and, on the other, to literature. One accepts the validity of the comparison, not by seeing it as a metaphor, equating subjunctively two disparate entities, but only by identifying indicatively the response to nature and to literature as one and the same. The homology borders on identity: "Brilliant writing radiates in the garden of literature in much the same way."

One might posit, by way of contrast, a poetics of correspondence (which one finds in Plato) alongside a poetics of resonance. In the first case, poetry establishes a truth through the sometimes allegorical, sometimes symbolic, sometimes metaphoric description of concrete details: the experience described and preserved in the poem always points to something else—whether moral truth, or aesthetic beauty, or romantic sentiment. The Western reader of Chinese poetry often searches in vain for the "point"—especially if she is reading in translation. The poem is not mimesis in either the Platonic or the Aristotelian sense; that is, it is not an imitation of ideal reality twice removed, nor is it the creation of the imagination. It is both the recording and the reenactment of an indicative moment, its realization in words.

For Chinese philosophers, truths are always contingent: one's

53

knowledge is always compromised. There is little or no desire to extrapolate human truths beyond human experiences, even if the cosmic experiences are explained in terms of familiar human realities. We might posit, on the one hand, the Dao (Tao) of existence and, on the other, the truth of life, and we might see a model of mimesis contrasted with a model of immanence. In the first instance, the model of mimesis, the unknown is conceived of as corresponding to the known and is real and valid the more that correspondence can be established and reiterated. In the second instance, the model of immanence, the only reality is whatever exists, whatever is, at the moment, now, thus. In the first instance, the Truth is adducible and achievable, if elusive; in the second instance, the Tao is ever present and yet not adducible. The Truth is replicable, accessible, and powerful: "Know the Truth and it will set you free." But the Tao is inimitable and fugitive and evanescent: "The Tao that can be said is not the commonplace and universal Tao."

My purpose in positing Chinese and Western polarities is to extend the basis for discussion, not from one vantage point or another, but from both. Our "horizon of expectations" must include more than one perspective; we must see from more than one reference point. The result will not be, as some indolent intellects too readily assume, a relativity of values, but a more rigorous, indeed, a more open, recognition of values with due acknowledgment of tacit premises. Each set of premises, what Stephen Pepper (1942) calls "world hypotheses," highlights another aspect of reality. As heirs to the traditions in both East and West, we are the beneficiaries of a multiple perspective, but along with the panoptic perspective is the challenge to check our own myopia. Myopia is not only ophthalmologic: in this day and age, that can be easily corrected. Intellectual myopia is more serious and more difficult to remedy. A bigot may have twenty-

twenty eyesight, and a blind man might be blessed with perfect "vision."

The virtues and the limitations of both traditions should become more apparent in any comparison. Our task is not to disown our own heritage but rather truly to discover it, by comparing it with another heritage, to see it in relief against the background of a different context. Too often what is accepted as universal is only customary and commonplace within the province that one inhabits. But commonplaces are not the same everywhere, and what is common to one may be uncommon to another. We can continue to pursue the mysteries, and we may even call our speculations the truth. What we discover may, in fact, be true given the facts on which we have based our theories. But, in the construction of any lasting theory, in the development of any durable understanding, analysis and intuition must proceed as one: the paradigms of mimesis must be alloyed with the paradigms of resonance.

I now proceed to "self-discoveries"—that is, reflections on the self that emerge from an exploration of the other. Because this discussion may be very abstract, I begin with an unexpected example, involving the translation into Chinese of an English nursery rhyme. I was once asked to check the Chinese version of

> *Jack be nimble Jack be quick,*
> *Jack jump over the candlestick.*

A simple enough assignment, to be sure. But when I saw the translation into Chinese, with *candlestick* correctly translated as *jutai*, I noticed an anomaly that had never troubled me before in English. My immediate response was that *jutai* was literally correct, but also somehow wrong. In Chinese, the nursery rhyme became absurd, more absurd than would be appropriate even for a nursery rhyme: who would be so foolish as to jump over a candle *holder?* Yet that is what the rhyme said. In remonstrating with the Chinese translator, I indicated that the word *candlestick* in the rhyme is implicitly interpreted by every speaker of English as a "candlestick" *with* a lighted candle. Contemporary speakers of English will, in reading *candlestick*, unwittingly supply the candle and the flame;[6] traditional interpretations place an even greater emphasis on the flame, if the following etymology can be credited: "For centuries, jumping over a candle has been both a sport and a way of telling fortunes in England. A candlestick with a lighted candle in it was placed on the floor. The person who could jump over it without putting out the flame was assured of having good luck for a full year" (Baring-Gould and Baring-Gould 1962, 194). The use of *candlestick* was, of course, dictated by the exigencies of rhyme, but the meaning in the rhyme is unmistakable, even if implicit. Yet what interests me about the example is that only an outside perspective forced me to see what an insider sees *through* and, seeing through, fails to notice.

Earlier, I mentioned that, when translated into Quechua, the phrase "Get thee behind me, Satan," required the equivalent of "Get thee in front of me, Satan"—deriving from the unimpeachable logic that the past is known (it is spread out, as it were, before one's eyes) but the future unknown (it cannot be seen and therefore is not before one's eyes). The logic of this made me think of Western preconceptions as illogical if we proceed from the same premises. However, they may be logical if we proceed from different premises. In what way does it make sense, I asked, to conceive of a future that is unknown to us as being in front of us, before our very eyes, and of the past, although known, as

6. The following sample of illustrated nursery rhymes all included a lighted candle in their versions of "Jack Be Nimble": *The Tall Book of Mother Goose* (1943, 35), *The Real Mother Goose* ([1916] 1944, 16), and *The Sesame Street Players Present Mother Goose* (1980, [82]). Richard Scarry's *Best Mother Goose Ever* ([1964] 1970, 3) shows the candle in the candlestick, but with no flame.

out of sight? I realized that the implicit paradigm in the Quechua mind-set was of someone standing *at rest*, whereas the implicit paradigm of Western preconceptions was of someone *moving forward*.

Only by such an implicit paradigm—of someone walking ahead—does it make sense to see the future as in front of us, even when we don't know what it is, and to see the past as behind us, even though we can look at it anytime we want. Does it seem significant that we more often and more naturally speak of facing the future rather than facing the past? Might it say something about the biases in our civilization that we value the future more than we value the past? We would rather speculate (subject to ocular inspection as well as to intellectual scrutiny) on the future than give due recognition to the past. Is the model of someone stationary necessarily inferior to the model of someone moving forward? Ordinary language preconceptions in English would suggest that it is. We believe that it is better to move forward than to stand still or to move backward. We believe that it is better to contemplate the future than to dwell on the past. We believe that—to paraphrase Scarlett O'Hara—"tomorrow is another [and presumably better] day!"

Perhaps the most unexpected self-discovery is to be made from the perspective of modern physics. One would think that physics is emblematic of the most objective, least subjective, intellectual pursuits: the study of material things, which traditionally does not admit of abstractions that cannot be scientifically measured. One would hardly go to physics for discoveries about the self. These days, however, physicists talk more like poets: in his celebrated popular exegesis of quantum mechanics, Gary Zukav writes, "The philosophical implication of quantum mechanics is that all of the things in our universe (including us) that appear to exist independently are actually parts of one all-encompassing organic pattern, and that no parts of that pattern are ever really separate from it or from each other" (1979, 47–48).

This formulation would seem to reinforce the Chinese or Confucian notion of the self as a nexus of human relationships that connects each of us with thousands, perhaps millions of ancestors and progenitors and with a potentially vast number of offspring. The description by Zukav (and others) of the physical world interpreted through quantum mechanics is strikingly filial in its orientation: "The physical world . . . is not a structure built out of independently existing unanalyzable entities, but rather a web of relationships between elements whose meanings arise wholly from their relationships to the whole." Among the many "weird" postulations of the new science, Zukav cites the "many worlds interpretation of quantum mechanics," which "says that different editions of us live in many worlds simultaneously, an uncountable number of them, and all of them are real." The new science has adopted some of the stances of the Chinese, and we hear echoes of the linguistic conflation of *heart* and *mind* in Chinese when Zukav writes, "Religion has become a matter of the heart and science has become a matter of the mind. This regrettable state of affairs does not reflect the fact that, physiologically, one cannot exist without the other. Everybody needs both. Mind and heart are wholly different aspects of *us*" (1979, 72, 87, 88).

Even the teaching of writing as self-expression has undergone a sea change recently. For years, the process of writing was—erroneously, in my opinion—presented as a "feel-good" approach toward self-fulfillment. This slant on writing seemed to suggest that the greatest writers were the most self-centered, the most self-indulgent. It left out writing as a discipline, writing, not as a solipsistic verbal display, but as a rigorous dialectical activity— writing as disciplined self-discovery. This point was emphasized in a piece some years ago in *College English* by Joseph Harris, which considered Roland Barthes, a French deconstructionist critic, and William Coles, a teacher of writing, who published a book called *The Plural I* in 1978. Harris's comments are directly relevant to our effort to discover ourselves through the study of others and provide yet another reinforcement of my theme, that the discovery of our selves depends crucially on our ability to understand and to recognize the other. Again, the divisions between subject and object are dissolved in the process of semantic—if not nuclear—fusion. "The task of the teacher of writing," Harris reminds us, "is not to train students to make their prose ever more Clear and Efficient. Neither is it to simply encourage them to be Expressive and Sincere. Rather it is to set up a situation that dramatizes the forces at work in writing. . . . It is to suggest that to reduce the complexities of writing to a single demand to be personal or to be clear is to trivialize it, that good writing is not simply writer-based or reader-based, but something of both" (1987, 168).

The discovery of the self in the singular turns out to be an illusion, and the question that I asked facetiously at the outset can now be answered seriously: If one is constantly in search of one self, who or what is doing the searching? Does it make sense for the self to search for itself? The answer, however, requires a reformulation of the question. If one takes what is called *the self* as multiple and plural rather than single and singular, the answer becomes clear, even if language makes it hard to formulate. For one can say that the selves of which we are conscious set out in pursuit of other selves as yet undiscovered. We are, each of us, composed of a virtual infinity of selves, perhaps as numerous as the number of our progenitors since the beginning of our evolution. Harris tells us that, for both Coles, the teacher of writing, and for Barthes, the literary aesthete, "the voice of a writer is always a weaving of other voices; the self is seen not as an isolated whole but as an amalgam of other selves, voices, experiences."

Our discussion of the Confucian notion of self, as an interstice in an elaborate network of human relationships, finds an echo in Harris's citation of Barthes: ""The image of the text Barthes continually returns to is that of a network, 'woven entirely with citations, references, echoes, cultural languages . . . which cut across it through and through in a vast stereophony. . . .' As Barthes writes in *S/Z:* 'This "I" which approaches the text is itself a plurality of other texts.'" Harris's conclusion resonates with the strategy of "seeing with another I": in our search for other worlds, we must start by realizing that, as Harris insists, "we are what our languages make of us and what we can make of our languages" (1987, 161, 169). The use of the plural form *languages* is the key to a proper understanding of the complexity of the self, which we must now view as a complex of selves subsumed in that unitary concept, *the self.*

As a final exercise in "seeing with another I," I offer a puzzle, which will serve as a parable for ways in which we can expand our vision even as we multiply the individual selves that compose the "I" that each of us uses to designate a self. The puzzle goes as follows:

> There are three men in a room, each with a hat on his head.
> Each is allowed to see the hats on the other two, but he is not
> allowed to take off his own hat. The three are all told that
> there are altogether five hats available, three blue, two red.
> The first person is asked if he knows the color of his own hat.
> He looks at the other two, then says he doesn't know. The
> second person is asked the same question: he doesn't know
> either. The third person is blind. He is asked the color of the
> hat on his own head. He knows. The question is, What color
> is the hat on the blind man, and how does he know?

I leave it to the reader to work out the puzzle. (A solution, however, is provided as an appendix for the skeptical.)

The point of this puzzle is that the blind man is able to "see" what his two sighted colleagues cannot know: the color of his own hat. One could speculate on the irony of a blind man "seeing" more than those with sight, but that would miss the point. The point is that the blind man "sees" what the eyes of his two companions see, and that insight allows him to know more than they do. It is also important to notice that merely borrowing their sight is not enough to solve the puzzle: the blind man also puts himself in the minds of the other two in order to arrive at his conclusion. Not only does he figure out what his colleagues see and don't see, but he also puts himself in their place, he "envisions" himself in their positions, he imagines himself as the other two, putting his "I-as-self" into their "I-as-self," imagining what their experience as the subjective first-person I would be. He borrows not only their eyes to see what they see; he also borrows their subjective first-person I to determine what it is they know or don't know. In this puzzle, the blind man cannot see through his own eyes, but he sees very accurately through the "eyes" and the "I's" of the others.

If a blind man can do this, how much more can we see through another I? How many other worlds might we discover in our search for the multiple selves in that consciousness to which we refer routinely as "I"? And how many "I's" might each of us find in our individual selves if we could project our view past our own provincial horizons to a larger perspective. We who have sight must not miss the chance to develop vision. The blind man in the puzzle shows us the difference between sight and vision. The Bible has identified those who have eyes and yet do not see: the blind man shows us how to see through another I.

There are many approaches to seeing with another I. The blind man used deduction; saints use creative sympathy; prophets use intuition; scientists use imagination. Shakespeare saw through many another I: whether it was Juliet, or Shylock, or Macbeth, or the three witches; Einstein imagined what it was like to be light and imagined it as both particle and wave. Chess players are the more successful the more they are able to figure out what their opponents are thinking. One of my favorite examples of how *not* to see from another I stems from the early days of the United Nations and involves Warren Austin, who was the first U.S. ambassador to the United Nations. When the debate between the Arabs and the Israelis became particularly acrimonious, Austin was said to have tried to moderate the overheated tempers by saying, "Gentlemen, gentlemen, can't we settle this matter in a Christian spirit?" Assuming that Jews and Muslims can be persuaded to act in a Christian manner is seeing through another I blindly.

We may be neither saints nor geniuses, but we can avoid the brutish insensitivities of ethnocentric mediators and develop a capacity for sympathetic and empathetic imagination. Conflict resolution can succeed only if the opposing sides begin to understand the other's point of view as well as they understand their own.

CHAPTER FOUR

Literati and Illiterati: Continuities in the Oral and Written Traditions

> Illiterate him, I say, from your memory.
> MRS. MALAPROP, from Richard Brinsley Sheridan, *The Rivals*

A long with many people who have to write a paper, prepare a presentation, or outline a complex mass of material, I have the habit of organizing the notes that I have been jotting down for weeks, and blocking out on a piece of paper, A, then leaving some space, B, and then leaving more space, C. In doing that, and before I had actually transferred the various items in my notes to one of these categories, I had—in a sense—designed my paper, given shape and organization to some rather miscellaneous thoughts. I had conceptualized what my talk would look like even before I had decided on the actual words I was going to use. Schematically, it was as simple as A-B-C.

On another occasion, I was running a computer disinfectant program to check for viruses in the files that I have on my hard disk—which total more than 250. The monitor flashed the name of each file in milliseconds as it scanned all my documents. As I watched this process and thought of the different kinds of files I have on my hard disk, I mused on the order I would use if I were to check out the files—in the order of chronology, from the most to the least recent or from the least to the most recent; in the order of size, from the largest to the smallest or in reverse; or perhaps in the order of importance. As I pondered these options, I noticed a pattern in the names of the files flashing on the monitor. Of course, without so much as asking, the computer was checking out my files—in alphabetical order. For its purposes, one order was as good as any other. In the time that it would take me to make a decision on which order to use, the computer was already well on its way to finishing the job by automatically adopting alphabetical order. It didn't matter in this case which order was adopted: there are times when the order doesn't really matter, so long as there is an order. How many times, when we need to cite a list of names, have we resorted to alphabetical order to avoid any semblance of bias? The alphabet provides an immediately available arbitrary and determinate sequence: its very arbitrariness is sometimes useful.[1]

I cite these two instances to indicate how ingrained alphabetical thinking is in the way we organize our lives, in the way we go about our business. The modern world is dominated not only by the alphabet but by alphabetical thinking. "Everything from A to Z," we say colloquially, scarcely conscious that we have just divided everything—at least in English—into twenty-six categories. Even the Almighty, at least in the Greek text of the Bible, speaks in an alphabetical language: "I am Alpha and Omega," the Almighty says in John's Revelation, "the first and the last, the beginning and the end" (22:13).[2]

1. One might think that the Frank Zappas and the Zimmermanns might take issue with this, but the propensity to begin with *A*'s might be deemed a disadvantage for those who would rather not "break the ice"; people with last names beginning with *Z* might find it advantageous to bring up the rear, particularly if they need more time for preparation.

2. An exact metaphoric translation of this quote, given the fact that omega is the last letter of the Greek alphabet and *Z* is the last letter of the English alphabet, should be, "I am the A and the Z, the first and the last, the beginning and the end."

For the better part of the world, literacy means—as my examples at the outset suggest—alphabetical literacy. But there are written languages that do not involve the alphabet. Consider a dictionary that is not in alphabetical order. Try designing a telephone directory without an alphabet. Imagine an index without an alphabet. Written languages that are analphabetical, that is, without an alphabet, have been invented: Chinese is one of them. In his book *The Alphabet Effect*, Robert Logan attributes to the lack of alphabet in Chinese the failure of that civilization to develop Western-style logic, or science, or codified law, or the concept of individuality. The impulse in Chinese, Logan (1986, 57) points out, is dialectical rather than deductive, analogical rather than logical. What Logan argues is that the thought-shaping template in the family of written languages that derived from the Phoenician alphabet through Greek and Latin has enhanced the development of many features of society that we recognize as peculiarly modern or Western.[3]

Most of the alphabets in the world can be traced to the writing system developed by the Canaanites around 3500 B.C. There are, however, four other systems: in addition to the Chinese, there are the writing systems of the Egyptians, the Harappa of the Indus valley, and the pre-Columbian meso-American Indians. Of these, all but the Chinese are extinct. By contrast to these writing systems, the alphabetical writing system is marked by two sig-

(In fact, two translations, the one published by the Watchtower Bible and Tract Society and another version by William Beck, do use "A and Z." I wonder how many readers of this passage, not knowing Greek, and thinking quite naturally of the letter *O* in English, are puzzled by the Lord presenting himself as Alpha and Omega, thereby suggesting that the beginning and the end are represented—not by the first and last letters in the alphabet—but by the first and the fifteenth letter of the alphabet.)

3. Logan's arguments are suggestive rather than totally persuasive: China, after all, developed a highly sophisticated science and technology well before the Renaissance, as Joseph Needham (1954–) has demonstrated; China has also had a long tradition of law, although it differs from the adversarial law that prevails in the West.

nificant advantages: it is, by far, the easiest system to learn (indeed, the Harappa writing system has yet to be deciphered [Logan 1986, 30]), and it is truly a phonetic notation system (as Havelock points out), not a mere syllabary, which does not separately identify consonants from vowels.

It may be simplistic to suggest that the very absence of an alphabet in Chinese culture is at the root of its difficulties in modernizing and in adapting to Western science and technology. But, if this is true, one advantage of the Chinese writing system should not be overlooked: it may be the key to the unparalleled continuity of Chinese culture, to the longevity of Chinese history. The written word in Chinese for *mountain* or *stream* or *peace* thousands of years ago is the same as it is today. The phonetics of Chinese have changed over the millenia, but not the graphemes, the written characters that embody the meaning. How many Western languages have lasted even as long as a thousand years? Speakers of modern English cannot read what Chaucer wrote, even though he lived a mere six hundred years ago. Americans have celebrated two hundred years of the Republic, but that's a far cry from the five thousand years of Chinese civilization.

In many ways, the modern world is a most remarkable, even an incredible world—full of inventions and technologies that only a century ago were unimaginable. But we haven't done very much to ensure our own survival or that of the planet. We think in terms of quarterly reports, in four-year election cycles, maybe even in decades: we have begun to think about the next century only in the last few years. We talk about the twenty-first century, but only dreamers and science fiction writers are concerned about the centuries beyond. How many of our policies are geared to the survival of our civilization for a thousand years, much less five thousand? What will our great grandchildren do when all the oil in the world is exhausted? In the 1980s, we spent almost ten times more money on defense than on education:[4] it is sad that the only thing former president George Bush asked us to read was—his lips. With our emphasis on defense over education, we may, in time, become the best defended country of dummies in the world. We respond to imminent crises, but give short shrift to long-term problems. Even if we succeed in resolving our present dilemmas, our uneducated—or poorly educated—children will be ill equipped to cope with the shifts and demands of new and unexpected developments in the next century. This is not an idle prophecy: look at all those who are being laid off today and ask yourself about the quality of their education thirty years ago. As educators, not only have we failed to reach those who can't read, but we have also failed to motivate those who *can* read and *don't*.

The declaration of 1990 as International Literacy Year was an occasion for reflection. Some viewed it as a celebration: if by way celebration we were intended to jump for joy at our achievements, I could not celebrate. We cannot celebrate literacy while there are populations living in poverty because they cannot read; we cannot celebrate literacy or congratulate those who *are* literate when much of the mischief in the world today was originated by populations who *can* read. There are too many people who have been trained to read, but somehow forgot to learn how to think. We have a tendency to think of reading as a passive skill and of writing as an active skill. But, if one is properly engaged, reading is active: it takes imagination and intuition to make the words on the page come alive. And we are wrong to think that merely by writing something, just because we are engaged in

4. The estimates from the Office of Management and Budget for 1989 were $298.3 billion, or 26 percent of the federal budget, for defense and $36.4 billion, or 3.2 percent of the budget, for education.

67

moving our hands, our fingers on the keyboard or grasping a writing instrument—that what we write is necessarily active. Indeed, that's what's wrong with a good deal of writing: there are too many passive writers around. The words are written or typed, but there is no active intelligence behind them, no sense of what the audience reaction to the words would be, no idea of the rhetorical effect of what is being said. Good, active writing is psychologically dynamic: it has the feel of good conversation, the presence of alert minds engaged in intellectual exchange. The quality of our thinking depends on the quality of our discourse, both oral and written.

In the literature on literacy, the ability to read is presented implicitly as an unmitigated good. The implication is that illiteracy is a blight that must be removed from the face of the earth. Certainly, in our print culture, the inability to read is a great disadvantage. But people make a mistake when they equate literacy with intelligence and illiteracy with a lack of intelligence. The invention of script—about which Plato, incidentally, had his suspicions—also has its downside. Our memories do not have to be as active as those of preliterate peoples, whose memories, by modern standards, were formidable. Before print, even scholars who could read had what we would regard as prodigious memories. To know a book in ancient times was to recall every word of it more or less verbatim (although it should be stipulated that "verbatim" in oral cultures is not exactly "verbatim" in script societies). We who have externalized our memories, and can retrieve information from dictionaries, encyclopedias, libraries, and now hard disks, CD-ROMs, and data bases, are freed from this burden on our brain. We need what I call *second-order memories:* we may not remember a fact, a detail, or a text, but we do need to recall where and how we can retrieve any fact, detail, or text. The challenge to our memory is not insuperable—although, for some, it is no mean feat to remember all the key codes that define one's existence: a computer network password, the four digits of an ATM PIN (automated teller machine personal identification number), a long-distance access telephone number, a login code, an e-mail address, a social security number, a zip code, an area code, not to mention the combinations to our safes.

(A modern analogy to the downside of script would be automatic dialing, which is a marvelous convenience, if one happens to be at the instrument where a frequently dialed number is programmed. However, if one is not at one's accustomed place, one has difficulty recalling even the most routine number. Before automatic dialing, frequently called numbers would have been impressed into the memory by constant repetition, and one would never have to "look up" a number one calls all the time.)

The alphabet has freed us from physical bonds, from the tyranny of the random, and from the limitations of human memory, for writing a thought down releases our minds for other things. We do not have to retain the whole history of our culture in our heads; thus freed from retrieving the past, we are at liberty to speculate creatively about the future. Through writing, we have access to posterity. Plato may have lamented the advent of writing as a threat that would undermine the human capacity to memorize, but the irony is that his influence on human civilization was made possible by the preservation of his thoughts, the transcription of what he said, on tablets, scrolls, codices, vellum, papyrus, foolscap, and paper.

The more I ponder the question of literacy, the more I realize how fascinatingly complex it is. I wonder if I am in agreement with the principles of the International Literacy Year. Am I in favor of teaching everyone to read? Of course I am. Will teaching people to read solve the world's problems, as some seem to think? I don't really know, but I do know that, unless everyone can read, the chances of any success in solving our problems are severely diminished. What is it, then, that makes me uneasy about literacy? In what way is it complex?

There are three kinds of confusion surrounding the question of literacy. The first involves *status*. The popular view of literacy is that it marks a higher social status: there is an erroneous belief that someone who can read is not only *better off* but *better* than someone who can't. Those who can't read are made to feel ashamed, as if they were somehow unworthy. Some illiterates enroll in "speed reading" courses because they want to avoid the stigma of confessing that they don't know how to read. But the true value of literacy is functional, not social; it is potential, not actual: it provides access to worlds that cannot otherwise be explored. Merely being literate isn't enough, no more than merely having legs. Only when one exercises literacy can one reap its benefits: we appreciate our legs most when we stand, or walk, or run, or dance. Having legs, being literate, is nothing to be proud of, although we may be grateful for both; what's important is what we do with what we have. There are too many with legs who don't exercise them, whose lives are spent "vegging out" before the television, whose only exercise is the trip to the refrigerator for another beer. There are too many among the literate population who know how to read, but won't, until finally their ability to read diminishes and they require easier and easier sound bites of information to sustain their short attention span: they are what I call *the self-disabled*.

I recall a story in the *Analects*, which tells of a worldly and successful disciple of Confucius visiting Yüan Xian, the master's favorite pupil. Yüan Xian was living as a humble scholar, but, when his well-to-do colleague asked him why he was poor, Yüan Xian replied: "I am poor, but I am not destitute." We should not forget the distinction: illiterate people are poor, but they are not destitute. They merely lack the means, not the resources, for education. And the resources that I have in mind are native intelligence, hope, courage, dignity, self-respect, fortitude, will, patience, perseverance, and character. There are some illiterates who have these resources in abundance, and there are some literates who lack them entirely. We should not confuse economic poverty with cultural poverty. Poor people are often very rich in cultural resources, just as some rich people are entirely lacking in some of these resources.

The second kind of confusion about literacy involves *value:* the similarity of *literacy* and *literature*, of the word *literate* and the word *literary*, conveys the plausible but mistaken notion that literacy is a precondition for literature and that only the literate can produce literature. This may be true in most cases, but it is definitely not true for all. Not all the writings of the literate have literary value: just recall the last contract you signed, or the last sales promotion that came in the mail, or the last administrative memo you read. But the reverse is true, although not many people think of it. We should not forget that our literate culture owes much to the *il*literati, to those who could not read, yet contributed to our literature. Most of these "unlettered" geniuses are shrouded in anonymity: since they had no access to transcription, they are lost; we can identify only a very few. They are the authors of the proverbs and the traditional folk songs, the storytellers who elaborated the myths and legends that shape every society. There are the oral traditions that produced the books of the Old Testament that circulated for years before being transcribed, as well as the several versions of the Christ story that we read in the Gospels. Even that oral poet so revered by the literati, the "author" of the *Odyssey* and the *Iliad*, whom we know by the name of Homer, was, legend tells us, unlettered, a blind bard who could neither read not write. Many of the sources of the literary tradition came from known and unknown illiterati.[5]

The third kind of confusion about literacy involves *intelligence:* the word *illiterate* somehow sounds unpleasant, like an illness. If the word *literacy* is neutral in sound, *illiteracy* is decidedly negative. Now we have all met snobs in the academy who believe that membership in the "School of Letters" automatically certifies a superior intelligence. Some of these very educated people are, if truth be told, not very smart. Indeed, I have sometimes wondered how it is possible that all that learning, all that knowledge, all that education, should make so small a dent. Unfortunately, much learning does not always make a person the more wise. Conversely, there are some uneducated people who are brilliant. A music professor friend of mine, one trained in the classical composers, who teaches sight-reading, composition, and the theory and history of music, tells me about Milt Jackson, who plays the vibraphone in the Modern Jazz Quartet. Jackson can't read a score, but he can memorize a piece of music in one hearing and play it faithfully thereafter; furthermore, his improvisational ability—which is, after all, the ability to *compose spontaneously*—is unequaled. Although he can't read music, who would dare call Milt Jackson a musical illiterate? Still, we are grateful for musical notation, and for transcriptions of music, so that we can hear re-creations of Milt Jackson's spontaneous inspirations. We are also thankful for the instrument of the written word, which has rescued so many masterpieces of the past from oblivion. The written word enables us to enjoy the

5. Apt as the use of the Latin words *literatus* and *literati* was for Roman times, their unthinking use today masks a linguistic oversight, because these words refer only to a *male* reader and to *males* who read. A female who reads would have been designated *literata* in Latin, females who read *literatae*. When we use *literatus* and *literati*, we reflect the male-centered prejudice that restricted literacy to males in ancient times.

Milt Jacksons of the world even if we are not lucky enough to encounter them in person.

I teach comparative literature, and I am especially grateful for these legacies of the past, from all cultures. I am grateful to the unknown scribes who copied down Plato's dialogues; I am grateful to whoever decided to write down the wonderful stories of the Bible; I am grateful for the versions we have of the great oral sagas of the world, from the Mayan *Popol Vuh* to the *Nibelungenlied* to the *Upanishads*. On this occasion, I would like to share with you a few of these treasures of literature, which I have selected because in one way or another they relate to the question of literacy. One comes from China two thousand years ago, another from Japan a thousand years ago, and the third from England a hundred years ago.

In the early Han dynasty, the son of a court historian in China was involved in some rather bad advice to the emperor: the emperor's displeasure was such that he imposed the severest penalty—either death or castration. For most scholars raised in the Confucian tradition of that time, both sentences were especially ignominious because each prevented the miscreant from fulfilling the filial obligation to his ancestors, which was to continue the family line. The condemned usually committed suicide since it, at least, represented an act of contrition. Castration, on the other hand, was a living shame, a reminder of continuing cowardice, and an abandonment of any procreational possibilities. Yet, despite this almost insupportable disgrace, the historian Sima Qian (Ssu-ma Ch'ien) (145–85 B.C.) opted for castration instead of death because he wanted to complete the history that his father had started and that he was obliged to finish. His defense deserves to be quoted at some length:

> A man has only one death: it may be as heavy as Mount T'ai [Tai], or as light as a feather. . . . A man of parts does not

disgrace his ancestors, or himself, or the ties of affection; but to violate the commandments . . . is shameful; to change one's dress for the red robes of the condemned is shameful; to be plucked bald and put in irons is shameful; to have one's flesh mutilated or one's limbs cut off as punishment is shameful; but of all these punishments, the vilest is to suffer castration. . . . But, if I privately endure my miserable life, closeted away in the depths of my vileness without escape, it is because there are things in my heart which are not exhausted by my baseness, which have not been expressed to the world, nor communicated to the generations to come. The number of precious treasures of the past, notice of which has been erased, is beyond calculation. . . . I proposed to entrust myself to my feeble words, to recapture all those things lost in ancient legend, to explore their processes, relate ends to beginnings, and to transcribe an account of success and failure, fortune and misfortune. . . . But before my draft could be finished, I met with this calamity. I regretted that I might not live to finish it, so I submitted to the extreme penalty without qualm. When, in fact, I complete this work, I shall deposit it in the "mountain archives," so that it will be transmitted to posterity and communicated to the great civilizations of the future. That will absolve me of my former disgrace, and though I suffer a thousand tortures, what would I have to regret?
(Watson, 1961, xii)

The annals and biographies and accounts that Sima Qian wrote, and for which, by living in utter ignominy, he sacrificed his life, became the first in a series of books that record the events in each of China's twenty-four dynasties, a record that covers over two thousand years of Chinese history—a continuous account unmatched in the world. Never was the power of the written word so manifest.

My second example comes from Japan, a thousand years after Sima Qian. The author of *The Tale of Genji*, the first and still one of the greatest novels in the world, was a lady-in-waiting in the elegant Heian court of the tenth and early eleventh centuries. She was known as Lady Murasaki. As a woman she was discouraged from learning the literati language of classical Chinese, which Japanese scholars of the time used in their literary compositions, so she resorted to writing in the vernacular—a medium considered beneath the dignity of her literary male contemporaries. Yet the work that she wrote, *The Tale of Genji*, has survived for a thousand years, delighting generations of readers—most of whom, given the scarcity of females among the literate population, were male. In one key passage, she has Genji, the prince who is the central figure of the novel, comment on the impulse of writing our life experiences down on paper: if we assume that the sentiments of her character, Genji, reflect her own thinking, then Lady Murasaki thought that the impulse to write down our lives came from

> the storyteller's own experience of men and things, whether
> for good or ill—not only what he has passed through himself,
> but even events which he has only witnessed or been told
> of—has moved him to an emotion so passionate that he can
> no longer keep it shut up in his heart. Again and again
> something in his own life or in that around him will seem to
> the writer so important that he cannot bear to let it pass into
> oblivion. There must never come a time, he feels, when men
> do not know about it. (Waley 1960, 501)

The literary value of Lady Murasaki's work far outstrips the literary creations of her male counterparts: it has endured as literature when their erudite literary compositions have been forgotten: their writings survive, but hardly anyone reads them. Lady Murasaki would have been considered "illiterate" by her male peers; they thought the vernacular she used "debased." But her writing was active, theirs passive. She invested her life and her imagination in what she wrote; they tried merely to be "correct" and clever, leaving nothing of their lives in their compositions. Literature is writing—in whatever medium, the literary language or the vernacular—that has life.

My third example comes from the most compassionate and egalitarian of all novelists, Charles Dickens. In *Great Expectations*, he has Pip say, "Much of my unassisted self . . . I struggled through the alphabet as if it had been a bramble-bush, getting considerably worried and scratched by every letter. After that, I fell among those thieves, the nine figures, who seemed every evening to do something new to disguise themselves and baffle recognition. But, at last I began, in a purblind groping way, to read, write, and cipher on the smallest scale" (1963, 53–54). Pip's struggles with the alphabet and his encounters learning the numbers remind us how arbitrary these systems of order are. The narrator of *Great Expectations* starts out as an illiterate, and, in acquiring literacy, he also seeks and finds his fortune. The irony of the work is that it is a literary masterpiece narrated by someone only recently "lettered." Pip's quote reminds us of the importance of memorizing the alphabet and the decimal numbering system. In the hegemonic and Eurocentric celebrations of Western culture, in the "cultural literacy" campaigns of the Allan Blooms and the E. D. Hirsches of the world, perhaps one shouldn't forget that the alphabet—without which there would be no Western civilization—came from Phoenicia and that the numbers we calculate with—without which there would be no Western science—derived from Arabia. Where would Western culture be without the contributions that came from Asia Minor, from the Akkadians, and from Sumer? Where would Western science be had it always kept itself purely Western? How far would mathematics have progressed if we still used Roman numerals instead of Arabic?

But, if we celebrate these recovered treasures of the past, recorded in the written language and preserved for posterity, how many others were lost? How many works of intellect and imagination and inspiration disappeared with the passing of the illiterati who were not fortunate enough to have their works transcribed?

I have taken pains to differentiate between literacy and illiteracy, between alphabetical and nonalphabetical literacy, and between literality and orality. While I would not promote *il*literacy, neither do I believe that we should neglect the contributions of the unlettered populations to culture. Although we are more often impressed with the benefits of alphabetical literacy, I have suggested that nonalphabetical writing systems—like Chinese—have their strengths as well. And I have suggested that we who are literate need to sharpen our oral skills, not merely as rhetoric in the modern sense, as a means of persuading our listeners, but also in its traditional sense, as a form of discourse that reveals truths not otherwise accessible.

I conclude with an observation. No one reading these lines is illiterate. I want to remember those who cannot read these words. We need to include them in our company not only for their sakes but for ours as well. We need to do a better job of reaching out to them; we need to learn to speak well as well as to write well, to learn how to articulate in human discourse, on the cuff, and spontaneously, the way Milt Jackson articulates on the vibraphone.

"The number of precious treasures of the past, notice of which has been erased," Ssu-ma Ch'ien reminded us, "is beyond calculation." "There must never come a time," Lady Murasaki would say, "when people do not know what our experience of life is." There are many who, like Dickens's Pip, are struggling "in a purblind groping way, to read, write, and cipher." We must not permit Mrs. Malaprop or anyone else to "illiterate them from memory."

When we meet the Pips of the world, we must teach them to read, and to read actively. And when they have learned to read, we must urge them to write—and to write often.

You see, I have great expectations as well. I can't wait to read what they have to say.

CHAPTER FIVE

China and the United States: Reflections on the Old and the New

Thered has been a widespread myth about China and the United States: that the people of the two countries like each other. Even during the sealing off of China from 1949 to 1979, and despite radically different ideologies, there was never any doubt that the Chinese people and the American people did not share the hostility between their governments. I confess that I was skeptical about this myth in the early 1970s and attributed it to the exploitative tendencies of "friendship" organizations, chambers of commerce, and travel agents—but now I am no longer so sure.

Indeed, the affection between the two peoples of the two cultures strikes me as remarkably like that between members of alternate generations, that is, between grandparents and grandchildren. Even the remoteness of the two countries has tended to reinforce this generational longing for each other. Psychologists tell us the "generation gap" between children and parents is narrowed between grandchildren and grandparents. Although this characterization perhaps exaggerates the state of affairs for the two countries, for the purposes of our considerations here, I'd like to think of China as a grandparent culture and of America as a grandchild culture. In what follows, my own perspective is both personal and professional, for these are the cultures that come together in me: I live in the tensions and the resolutions between them. For the first part of my life, the grandchild and the grandparent were separated: they almost never met, and there was a distance between them that, frankly, made things rather difficult for me. But, lately, the situation has been better. I hope that it will become obvious, in the course of this chapter, that I love them both.

But love requires honesty, and what I have to say about both cultures will be as critical as it is admiring, for I want to explore the consequences of this myth about China and the United States, not to arrive at any political insights, but to explore some basic complementary belief systems about time and about our place in history. With a little luck, these ruminations may also have something to say to each of us and perhaps provide a fresh perspective on our own lives.

Let us look first at grandparents and grandchildren. The charm of grandparents is that they are usually benign and affectionate; the charm of grandchildren is that they are adorable—at least to their grandparents. But there is another side to youth and old age: senility is not charming, nor is puerility; old fogeys are not attractive, nor is adolescent behavior. Some years ago, a film was made about old age and dying—two very unpopular subjects in popular American culture. The film was called *On Golden Pond*, which, as it turns out, was Henry Fonda's last picture. It had a good run, and most people who saw it liked it. *On Golden Pond* represented for me a fascinating glimpse of the way in which Americans think about old people. Most Americans are not attracted to old people as they are, nor do we take notice when they act their age. But when they act young despite their age, if they are cantankerous and irreverent, even if they are childish and adolescent—as Henry Fonda's character was— the effect, for most Americans, is disarming. The movie *Cocoon* showed a similar emphasis: old people who find a fountain of youth and become like children again—break dancing with no damage to their brittle bones—these old folk seemed to belie their age. In other words, in the United States, what is important is to be young. Old age is something to be avoided: it is regarded as an unfortunate accident, something we can't do anything about, but, in any case, something we don't want to be reminded of.

Almost the exact opposite is true of the Chinese perspective on age. In *The Analects*, Confucius tells us, "At fifteen my mind was set on learning. At thirty my character had been formed. At forty I had no more perplexities. At fifty I knew the Mandate of Heaven. At sixty I was at ease with whatever I heard. At seventy I could follow my heart's desire without transgressing moral principles" (2:4). In other words, life gets better as we get older.

Americans seem to like old people who act like kids, and Chinese dote on children who act grown up.

American tourists have noticed how particularly attractive Chinese children are. Of course, children of any culture are very winning, each in their way, but the charm of Chinese children seems, somehow, different. I believe that it's because Chinese children are trying to act like little adults: they are trying so hard, so earnestly to act like grown-ups that there is something touching in the effort. The American tendency is to identify children with unbridled energy and zest, with mischievousness and irresponsibility, and, when these drives are barely under control, the sparkle of mischief just beneath the surface of a good upbringing, all hell about to break loose just as our backs are turned, the effect seems enormously touching and diverting. The Chinese have a phrase for what I am describing, and it has the sense of children who understand things, who are trustworthy and grown-up in their demeanor. For a child in China, it is a compliment to be called *laoshi*. The phrase consists of the words *lao* (old) and *shi* (reality). Together, they indicate qualities in a child who is honest and reliable, mature beyond her years. This is in no way what Americans would call "a goody-goody," or "a Little

Lord Fauntleroy," whom we might regard as a little prig, a tattletale, or "a Momma's boy." The Chinese *laoshi* is reminiscent of the French expression, "Sois sage," roughly translated as, "Be good." But, whereas the American version implies the negative—"Be good" usually means, "Don't be bad," or, "Stay out of trouble"—*laoshi* is positive, reflecting adult virtues in children, a certain moral precociousness that the Chinese find admirable in the young.

I have already mentioned that the calculation of one's age in China is based on a communal reference, the number of years one has lived in, and not on an individual time-scale, the actual time one has lived. There are very few in China who complain about this superannuation of age: no one suggests that it makes them out to be older than she is, and no Chinese is ashamed of her age. I find it amusing that many Americans think that they are complimenting Chinese when they say that they look younger than their years. For Americans, it's an embarrassment to look old. For Chinese, the opposite would be true—it's embarrassing to appear immature. Behavior is what counts: one should look as if one knows something about life.

There's even a T-shirt quite popular in the United States that proclaims proudly, "I refuse to grow up." Another has the motto, "You're only young once, but you can be immature for ever."[1] Neither of these shirts, I venture to say, would be very popular in any "old world" country. But, if we can deplore the puerility of much of American culture—consider, for example, how many adults in this country have the dubious charms of adolescence— we must also deplore the senility of the current regime in China. A 1990 bulletin from China, where all the top leaders were over eighty years old, tells us about the declining health of one of its

---

1. Might it be sententious to reverse this aphorism somewhat and insist, "You have a right to be immature once, but you can be young forever."

leaders, Vice President Wang Zhen. The item, from the *New York Times*, is worth quoting: "Wang Zhen, the 82-year old Vice President of China, has been hospitalized, according to the Associated Press in Beijing. . . . An unofficial report circulating in Beijing is that Mr. Wang, who was last seen in public Aug. 5, broke his leg when Peng Zhen, 88, the former chairman of the National People's Congress, fell on him. A former political commissar, Mr. Wang is a conservative ideologue who rose through the military and is considered one of the most outspoken hardliners in the Chinese Government" (27 October 1990). The Chinese leadership is giving new meaning to the phrase "toppling government leaders"; in this case, it is no mere metaphor but a literal description of how leaders fall. Although a few "youngsters" (those in their fifties) have been installed in power, things haven't changed very much, and new "old" people are replacing those who have passed away.

The challenge of combining vigor with wisdom, of experience with a fresh outlook, remains with us. There is a difference between being youthful and being infantile and between being wise and being wizened. And this is where the examples of the United States and China are particularly instructive, especially in contrast, for one represents the wisdom of the ages, the other the dynamism of youth.

The remarkable thing about China today is that it, somehow, survives.

I was once invited to talk about China to a kindergarten class in Bloomington, Indiana. A five-year-old asked me what the difference was between a Chinese revolution and other revolutions. My first inclination was to deny any difference; after all, revolutions are revolutions. But, as I scanned the history of China, I realized the depth of the question. In the twentieth century alone, China has had four revolutions—the overthrow of the monarchy in 1911; the overthrow of the literati in the

May Fourth Movements of 1919 and 1925; the overthrow of the Nationalists in 1949; and the overthrow of old institutions—the old guard, the old Party, the old culture—in the devastation known as the Cultural Revolution that began in 1966 and lasted ten years. And, with the failed uprising of 4 June 1989, it looks as if China isn't finished with revolutions yet. Contrast this with the revolutions in other countries: the United States has had only one, the Revolutionary War of 1775–83; there is only one French Revolution, and it raged from 1789–99; and there is but one Russian Revolution, and it occurred in 1917. The cataclysms that have rocked China on an average of once every twenty years would have rent the fabric of any other culture.

The durability of China as a cultural and national entity, its resilience to major disruptions, bears closer scrutiny. Nor is this a recent phenomenon. Over the last thousand years, northern China has been ruled by foreign powers for 510 years, or more than half that time, and the entire country has endured foreign rule for 357 years, that of the Mongols from 1279 to 1368 and the Manchus from 1644 to 1912. Yet China remains Chinese, not Manchu or Mongol. As a political organism for survival, even against foreign intrusion, as a perdurable idea that prevails over even continued and repeated subjugation by alien forces, China represents an instance of the political survival of a species that is unique. It is the counterpart in history to the coelacanth in biology.

The coelacanth is a fish that has survived at least from the Cretaceous period, seventy million years ago, when the giant reptiles, like the dinosaurs, roamed the earth. In terms of human history, the civilization that we know as China was contemporary with the great pharaohs of Egypt, the Periclean age of Ancient Greece, the civilizations of Babylon and Hammurabi. If cultural longevity is a measure of a civilization's strength, and even if

China becomes extinct in our time—which, despite her travails, is hardly likely—no country would measure up.

That is why the example of China is worth considering here in the United States, for we may well ask how long our civilization is going to last. How long is this youthful experiment in egalitarian creativity going to continue—merely into the next century or for centuries to come? Our notions of the future constitute science fiction, but our vision of the future does not very often involve a United States of America in the twenty-fourth or twenty-fifth century. Preposterous as these perspectives may be, consider the Chinese of the Han dynasty; they could, if they wanted, envision a culture that they could identify as their own two thousand years into the future. Can you imagine a world two thousand years from now that, were you to return, you could recognize as American?

To some, this speculation may seem fanciful. Some can barely see past the present decade, much less the next millennium. Besides, what does that future have to do with us? That the Chinese thought about the future in precisely this way can be documented. Of the many proofs that I can offer, let me cite but two.

Earlier, I mentioned Sima Qian, the author of the *Shiji* (The Historical Record); written in the first century B.C. in 130 chapters, the *Shiji* is still the definitive history of the Chinese people up to that time. Sima Qian placed his work in the "mountain archives"—two thousand years later we are still reading his words.

The second example of planning for the future is the scheme that the founder of the Ming dynasty (1368–1644) provided for the names of all his descendants. In Chinese, most family names consist of one character, given names usually two. Hence, the family name of the Ming was Zhu, and the founder's given name was Yuanzhang. Each of the three branches of the Ming imperial family was assigned one character that each generation had to share; in addition, the second character had to contain one of five "radicals." (A radical is a symbol that recurs in words of the same category: i.e., plant names would have the "grass" radical, words for articles of clothing would have either the "silk" or the "cloth" radical, etc.) The founder of the Ming determined that the generations should each be designated by names sharing one of the radicals for the five principal elements: fire, earth, metal, water, and wood, in that order. There are names for ten generations, and the scheme provides for members of each of the three branches of the family. Members of the same generation across the three branches could be identified because they would share the same radical, representing each of the five elements.

There are several salient points to make about this scheme. That such a scheme exists at all might be considered remarkable. Most people don't decide on the names of their children much before they are born. Very few are consulted when the names of their children's children are being picked. One marvels at the breathtaking perspective of the scheme, which encompasses three hundred years, if one allows for an average of thirty years per generation. In fact, this scheme was actually followed for 276 years!

This genealogy points out several attitudes that the Chinese have about identity. First, one's identity is determined by one's place in the family matrix; it does not depend on individual characteristics or the whimsy of one's parents. In a very real sense, one's identity, one's name, is largely determined by one's ancestors. Second, one's identity involves three coordinates: a person is designated in history by a form of genealogical triangulation: family, branch, and generation. Third, the scheme determines a hierarchy of importance: one is defined first and foremost by the family of which one is a member, then by the branch of the family to which one belongs, and, finally, by the generation in which one finds oneself.

The social nexus in Chinese culture that determines one's identity may also be reflected in the act of self-naming, that is, the reference one makes to oneself. In most Western languages, this is not a problem: the simple first-person singular pronoun—whether *I*, or *je*, or *jo*, or *ich*—suffices. These are nominative forms, which designate the subject or agent of an action. If one wants to name oneself in the objective case, one has another set of first-person singular pronouns: *me* in English, *me* (muh) in French, *me* (meh) in Spanish, or *mich* in German. Chinese makes no such distinctions between nominative and objective case: the first-person reference is the same in both instances. Where it makes a distinction is in the social status of the self-reference, reflected in the practice of a self-effacing designation of oneself when addressing superiors, or the omission of any self-reference. In traditional China, a woman's first-person pronoun when addressing her husband was a self-deprecating *qie*, which was the word for concubine. A minister addressing the emperor would use *chen*, which derived from the word for subject or vassal and which came to mean both "minister" and the "I"-form that a minister used when addressing royalty. Petitions to the government by commoners would use a self-reference like *yimin*, which comprises the word for "ants" and the word for "people, subjects" of a country. In other words, these self-referential pronouns were determined by one's relationship with one's interlocutor. Although the egalitarian influence of Westernization has eroded the traditional courtesies, one sometimes encounters—especially in correspondence between educated people—such expressions as *yudi* (your humble younger brother), or *yuxiong* (your humble older brother), or *yujian* (as I—humbly—see it), or *yuyi* (my humble opinion). The other defines the self, and the self is determined by others.

Consider, for example, the order in which we address a letter: the name of the addressee is followed by the street and house number, then the town or city and the state, and, finally, the country. Wouldn't it be more practical were the order reversed, so that each succeeding postman would read down the address, until finally only the local postman would need to look at the name of the addressee? Is there any reason for the intermediary postmen to know the name of the person you're writing to? Yet this order, which reverses Western convention, is precisely the order in which letters are addressed in Chinese and Japanese: the country first, then the city, then the street address, and only then the name of the addressee.

If time and identity can be so differently conceived, so can the concept of place. What is our place in the world? It is clear from Confucian, Buddhist, and Taoist texts that we are not considered as the center of the universe. Confucius refused to speculate about the heavens, about the life hereafter, about anything beyond the world of human relations that he did not know. The Buddhists posited a world of endless duration: instead of calculating in years, decades, centuries, or millenia, they reckoned in terms of kalpas, with each kalpa lasting at least 4.23 billion years. The Taoists conceived of all phenomena being equal, with no being or creature or thing superior to any other.

But, if there is a sense of place in Chinese, the most influential was the Confucian concept of *ren*, often mistranslated as "benevolence," or "virtue," or, most awkwardly, "human-heartedness." While *ren* may produce feelings of benevolence, virtue, or human-heartedness, it is none of these three, but something more basic. The word comprises the words for "man" and "two," which can also be taken as indicating the "plural." The etymological sense of the word *ren* gives us the key to its meaning, for, by combining the word for "man" with the marker for plurality, *ren* reminds us that the essence of being human is our relatedness to other human beings; it reminds us that at least two other human beings are involved in our being, in our being human; it reinforces the sense of identity as being a part of a larger whole, like the interstice of a network. Each individual is regarded as the intersection of two strands; each of these two strands resulted from two other strands. Humanity, in this scheme, is made of a huge, intricate, reticular matrix. This is merely another way of saying that every human being has had—since the beginning of time—two biological parents.

The Chinese family tree is an intricate network, a genealogical organizational chart. At the center is the self, surrounded by relatives on the father's side and on the mother's side, extending to two generations above as well as two generations below. The I—the self—must refer to each relative by a separate term of address. In other words, it's not just "uncle," but "uncle-on-the-maternal-side-older-than-myself"; it's not merely "cousin," but "female-cousin-on-the-paternal-side-younger-than-myself." Each term of address is differentiated according to three distinctions: maternal/paternal; male/female; older/younger. To a society where even the nuclear family is fragmented, this five generational fabric may seem oppressive. In traditional China, this makeup of the family was no mere abstraction: homes often comprised members of five generations, and a sense of loyalty to the family was engendered not only by ties of mutual affection but by law. Crimes committed by any individual, of course, disgraced his family, but the family was implicated in more direct ways: punishments for severe crimes were extended beyond the miscreant to several degrees of relatedness and to more than one generation of the extended family, and, in the case of the most heinous crimes, even the most distant relatives were affected. "Your brother's keeper" was more than just a phrase.

All this was conducive to a concept of oneself as part of the fabric of humanity. One was never permitted to forget this fact. Selfishness was not merely a character flaw: it was an impiety against one's forebears. To be selfish was to deny the very basis of one's being, which is that one is descended from other human beings. The only reality was the fabric of the family through the generations, the only permanence, the only immortality, the continuation of that network from the beginning through to the end of time.

An individualist may find all this stultifying: certainly, it undercuts any notion of the self as a free spirit, at liberty to find herself, to follow her own destiny. From the Chinese, and specifically the Confucian, viewpoint, each one of us owes his life to others, and to give our lives to someone else is merely to repay the debt that we incur at the moment of birth. This sense of connectedness means that one rarely senses in China the existential loneliness that one encounters so often in modern-day America. In traditional China, there are poems of longing, of missing a loved one, but one is never lonely among people. Privacy—both word and concept—is virtually unknown among traditional Chinese. In many of the overcrowded countries in the Far East, privacy is not so much a right as a rare privilege, which only the rich and the powerful enjoy. Americans regard privacy as an inalienable right. But, for people who define their existence by their relatedness to others, privacy can also be a prison. Solitary confinement, after all, is the ultimate privacy. In traditional China, one's place was among people, and it was not demeaning, but rather reassuring, "to know one's place."

Some other contrasts in cultural perception—Thomas Kuhn might call them *paradigms*—can be easily illustrated, and their differences recognized graphically. The Western notion of individuality and the emphasis on the rights of the individual could be characterized as a series of concentric circles, with the self-ego-I at the center (see figure 1). The Chinese notion of self can be represented as a reticular model, where the self-ego-I is represented by the intersection of lines (see figure 2). We may call these *paradigms of the self*. Where one emphasizes an almost fortress-like integrity and self-sufficiency, the other reminds us of the fragility of our existence: the resemblance of the genealogical network to an intricate spider's web is not totally fortuitous.

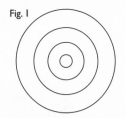

Fig. 1

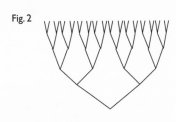

Fig. 2

Along with these models, I mention two others that graphically represent certain strains of thought in modern America and in traditional China. We may label these *paradigms of reality*. In the one case, there is a Manichaean division of equal portions of black and white in a rectangular box (see figure 3). This figure represents a view of reality as a series of confrontations, of diametric oppositions: the fight between good and evil, the good guys versus the bad guys. Us/them distinctions reflect this paradigm. Politicians use this model because it appeals to those who are too lazy to think. The Chinese, and specifically Taoist, view of reality, however, is represented by the now familiar symbol of bipolar complementarity (see figure 4). The ironies implicit in this paradigm are worth analyzing: note that in the center of the black portion there is a white dot and that in the center of the white portion there is a black dot. This reminds us that, in some ways, the greatest enemy is the enemy within. Note also that the dividing lines are curved, not straight, and that there is a sense almost of supple nurturing implicit in the configuration: pictures of fetuses in the womb, with the big head and the beady eyes, always remind me of this model. The curved lines are not confrontational but defining and somehow enveloping. One notes that there is a perfect "fit" between the black portions and the white portions of the symbol: it reminds us that the principle of reality and of life is the creative fusion of opposites. The Chinese are not averse to seeing this symbol as a graphic representation of the physical intercourse between male and female: of course, they call it *yin* and *yang*. Long before the feminist movement, the Chinese recognized that every human has elements of both the male and the female and that no one is completely one or the other.

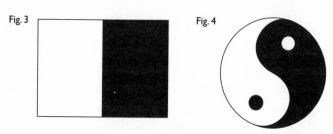

Fig. 3   Fig. 4

If we examine these four models, of identity and of reality, and reflect on the complexities of modern life, it must become obvious to us that the atomistic model of the self is no longer as convincing as it is often thought to be. We need to be reminded time and time again of John Donne's famous dictum, from his *Devotions on Emergent Occasions*, which I should like to quote at some length: "No man is an island, entire of itself; every man is a piece of the continent, a part of the main. If a clod be washed away by the sea, Europe is the less, as well as if a promontory were, as well as if a manor of thy friend's or of thine own were: any man's death diminishes me, because I am involved in mankind, and therefore never send to know for whom the bells tolls; it tolls for thee" (1959, 108). I am struck by the phrase referring to "a clod . . . washed away by the sea." There are times when I wish that clods I have known would be washed away by the sea. But Donne reminds me that, even if we divest ourselves of these clods, we are the less. It may surprise you to know that this most Christian of texts is the perfect Western exposition of the Confucian concept of *ren*. For *ren* reminds us that we are part of the continent of humanity. Donne's formulation is as fresh today as it was in the seventeenth century, except today we might not restrict the metonymy for humanity to Europe. The profound truth of this Christian and Confucian paradox is that we cannot "isolate" the enemy completely: that the people we despise, the enemy that torments us, cannot be removed without some diminution in us. Troublesome as it may be, we cannot get rid of even the most despicable people without bearing some of the responsibility ourselves. Walt Kelly's Pogo said the same thing, but in a characteristically self-ironic American accent: "We has met the enemy, and it is us!"

The Taoist symbol also reminds us of paradox as a principle of life. There can be no life without death, no up without down, no good without evil. Its model of reality is nonlinear. In America, it is significant that, along with the refusal to accept old age—many, like Jack Benny, would like to be thirty-nine forever—there has been a reluctance to accept the fact of death. I like to tell my students to take out a coin whenever they are confronted with the loss of a loved one. I ask them if they've ever seen a one-sided coin (I don't mean a coin with two heads, I mean a coin with only one side). I ask them if they have ever encountered life that did not also involve the reality of death. And then I ask why we begrudge someone her death if we do not begrudge her her life. We know, but choose to forget, that one makes the other possible. Without life, there is no death; without death, there can be no life. When we protest someone's death, are we not looking at one side of the coin and cursing the other side?

These notions may seem banal enough and obvious to everyone. Yet I submit that this paradoxical model is not often encountered. What we usually get is a millenarian, linear model of reality, a progressivist, onward-and-upward model, where tomorrow will be better than today just as today is better than yesterday. We sell futures on the future, and—in environmental pollution, in massive debts that our grandchildren must pay, in the proliferation of nuclear contamination—we are rapidly using up the future. We live in an environment of what I call *false ultimates*, in an era of unending hype. One of my favorite allegories in sports involves the interview that Tom Brookshier had with that moody, talented running back Duane Thomas just after he led the Dallas Cowboys to victory in the 1972 Super Bowl. Brookshier asked Thomas whether there was anything to compare with this experience of triumph. "Hey, Duane," Brookshier said, "Isn't this the 'ultimate' moment in sports?" To which Duane Thomas replied, with scarcely disguised impatience, "If it was the ultimate, why do they play the game again next year?"

It isn't only the media or the promoters or the advertisers who bombard us with the superiority of the new, the promise of tomorrow, and the blandishments of the future: our language inculcates this preference for what's to come in the words we use. I have always thought it unfair that the word *precede* did not have the same glamor as the word *succeed*. Our language subliminally persuades us that what comes after, what "succeeds," is what will be triumphant, what "succeeds." Indeed, we almost believe that *merely* coming after is a "success" and that the meanings of *successive* and *successful* are somehow related. The only counterparts that I can think of for *precede* and *predecessor* are phrases like *has-been, yesterday's news,* and *all washed up*. There is not as much appreciation for predecessors as for successors, and, with some rare exceptions, we have a tendency to forget where we come from. I believe that America has forgotten what made America great: what we need to learn from the Japanese are the lessons that they learned from Americans but that we have forgotten. The lessons that General Motors taught the world in the 1930s and 1940s were learned by the Japanese; these were the same lessons that the General Motors of the 1970s and 1980s forgot.

We often forget what got us where we are today. But, when we forget our past, we do more than betray our legacy; we betray ourselves.

I remember a story I heard when I was visiting a small town near Guilin in China, on the site of a canal that had been built hundreds of years ago. The canal project had been proposed to the emperor, and he assigned the task to the most able engineer he could find. But the engineer was not able to solve the many complex problems of geology and soil shift and hydraulics, and, as a result, he failed. The emperor had him executed. A second engineer was chosen to complete what the first engineer had begun, and although he benefited from the unsuccessful efforts of his predecessor, the complications proved too much for him as well. In time, he failed to accomplish his task and paid with his life. A third engineer was summoned, succeeding the first two, and he succeeded where the others had failed. By examining how his predecessors had failed, he was spared the mistakes that they made. He recognized that his chances of success were greater for him than for those who came before him because they had already tried out some of the alternatives that he might have considered. A plaque placed at the site of this canal honors this engineer, but it isn't so much to celebrate his achievements as to pay tribute to his moral character. The memorial tells us that, recognizing how much he owed his two predecessors, the third engineer decided to share their fate. He committed suicide. He could not enjoy the honors for which they had sacrificed their lives. This parable reminds me of the blind man's puzzle: this engineer, like the blind man, did not forget that he was the beneficiary of what other people saw.

Whether we like it or not, we are involved in humanity. Only some of us remember.

There are times when I think, particularly after 4 June 1989,

95

that China is sacrificing its future to preserve its past. It is not possible to travel in China without stumbling on historical artifacts almost everywhere. One of the ironies of the "modernization" movement in China today is that many of the most important and exciting archaeological discoveries made in the last thirty years were made, not by antiquarians digging up the past, but by civil engineers clearing the ground for the construction of a new building. The terra-cotta army of the first emperor, Qin Shihuangdi, was found in Xian in 1974; the two thousand-year-old-woman and the ancient manuscripts in Mawangdui, outside of Changsha, were unearthed in 1972 and 1973. Whenever ancient treasures are unearthed, of course, construction must be suspended, and a museum has to be built on the site. Indeed, the fastest growth industry in China has been tourism, and the major tourist attraction is China's ancient past. I don't know how many projects, designed to modernize China and its economy, have been halted or shelved because some precious portion of the past has been uncovered. Archaeology and modernization in China provide a novel twist to the French adage, *"Plus ça change, plus c'est la même chose"* (the more things change, the more they remain the same).

China appears to live off her past, just as America seems to live off her future.

The present-day pressures of overpopulation in China have led in the last decade to a state policy restricting families to one child only. The elaborate set of names, one for each relative in a five-generation scheme, that I cited earlier has become obsolete in our lifetime. These terms of address, this elaborate form of differentiating between older and younger, that has persisted for thousands of years will no longer exist when there are no older or younger brothers, no older or younger sisters to speak of. In time, if the policy is universally applied, all the children will be only children.

It is these only children who concern me. Without the balancing presence of sibling rivals, without an institutionalized respect for the elder (since the terms for "elder brother" and "younger brother" will become obsolete), will the only children of the future become the egoistic, self-centered, spoiled exponents of a "me-first" generation? Will they be fierce individualists who will be difficult to absorb in a group, who will refuse to function as part of a team, who will see their families as obstacles to overcome, excess baggage to discard? And, if these children decide themselves not to have children, who will succeed them? Yet the pressures of overpopulation in China mandate these restrictions: there is no way to stabilize population growth with more than one child per family. But this "enlightened" policy has resulted in infanticide, when the "only" child was a female or retarded or deformed. Those who argue in favor of eugenics, allowing only "healthy" babies to survive, might consider the example of Helen Keller and Alexander Pope and Stephen Hawking—who triumphed despite enormous physical disabilities: their contributions to human culture are incalculable. We need not only the smarts of the modern but the wisdom of the traditional to navigate our way through these complexities.

I hope you will not misunderstand me when I say that I naturally see a future that is neither Chinese nor American. I'd like to think that the future will be, in a sense, Chinese American. I see a future that is both smart and wise; I hope to see in the citizens of the future both self-reliance and self-effacement; and I look forward to a time when the present borrows neither from the past nor from the future, a time when the past and the future are always present. We shall not forget our indebtedness to the past, nor shall we overlook our responsibilities to the future. We will always sense the ties that bind us to our predecessors and the commitments that we make to our successors. And, when we have accomplished this, we will not die, but live always, for, just as our ancestors live in us, so too we will live on in our progeny and in our effects. So it has been—we discover anew with every generation—and so it shall always be, for what has been old will one day be new and what was new once is already old. And we realize that old and new are not two things, but one, and that in the perspective of eternity we are as young as a newborn babe and as old as Methuselah.

CHAPTER SIX

The Three L's: Liberalism, Liberty, and the Liberal Arts

Let me take you on a road, a rambling road that encourages free and easy wandering, a road that meanders along the contours of the land. You need time for this road, as well as patience, and a good deal of imagination. It doesn't go directly to your destination, and there are pitfalls and byways that make it tough going, but it is, in the end, a road that may be worth traveling. Some call it the road to Serendip, where serendipity thrives; others think of it as the road to Oz, which leads to a wizard who is, and is not, a bag of wind; we might call this the road to L.

One of my favorite parables is from the Chinese writer, Chuang-tzu (fourth century, B.C.):

There was a man who made a salve to prevent chapped hands, which his family used generation after generation to bleach silk in water. A traveler heard about the salve and offered to buy the formula for a hundred measures of gold. "All these years, we have been bleaching silk with this salve, and earned only a few measures of gold," the man told his family. "Now, we can sell the formula and make a lot of money." So, the traveler bought the salve and introduced it to the king of a neighboring state. The king put the man in charge of his troops, and that winter he won an important naval battle, largely because he supplied his soldiers with the salve: their

> hands no longer chapped, the soldiers were much more
> effective with their weapons than the enemy. After the victory,
> a portion of the conquered territory was awarded to the man
> as his fief. Now, the salve prevented chapped hands in either
> case; but one man used it to get a fiefdom, while the other
> never got beyond bleaching silk. (Watson 1968, 34–35)

There is a modern counterpart to that story: the scientists at the Minnesota Mining and Manufacturing Company, 3M, which is famous for making Scotch Tape, had been working for many years on developing the strongest glue in the world, a super glue that would replace rivets, nuts and bolts, nails and screws. One of the concoctions that the 3M laboratories came up with was an adhesive that was so weak that it took no effort at all to pry apart the things bonded together. As super glue, it was a complete flop, a waste of time and money. But then Art Fry, a 3M chemical engineer, came up with a bright idea and decided to package little pads of paper with this glue on one edge. These slips of paper are now ubiquitous—we use them as notes and reminders, sticking them on refrigerators, on letters, on doors: they have a thousand and one uses. We know them as "Post-its," a product that now makes more money than any other for 3M.

Students who overemphasize grades are like the chemist who develops a weak super glue and fails to see the possibility of Post-its. They have been merely bleaching silk, without seeing the possibility of a salve. Many people get good grades but grade out poorly in life. That's because they fail to realize that the object was to learn, not just to get a good grade: the important test is how one grades out in life. The question is, Do you see the salve for bleaching silk, or for winning a fiefdom? Do you see the adhesive as bad super glue or as the key to Post-its?

College students seek a liberal education, one that trains them not just how to study, how to retain what they study, how to take examinations, how to write papers, but also, presumably, *how* to think. This is particularly important these days because there are more and more people who, not content with teaching young people how to think, insist on telling them *what* to think. These self-appointed authorities will define for anyone willing to listen the "core tradition of Western civilization." Womens studies, ethnic studies, non-Western courses, are, for these intellectual reactionaries, not in the core tradition.

This appeal is usually supported by two arguments: first, that we should know our intellectual and cultural roots and, second, that only the study of Western civilization can teach students how to think. Like all plausible arguments, these statements are both true and untrue. The advocates of "back to basics," those who oppose what they see as the "dilution" of the liberal arts, fail to point out the part that is untrue. Yes, it is true that we should know where we have come from to find out where we are and where we are going. That part no one doubts. But not all of us derive from the so-called Judeo-Christian tradition, not all of us are descended from those who came over on the May-flower, and not all of us are males. When historians think of the progenitors of the Western tradition, they think only of those who fathered us, rarely if ever of those who mothered us. I completely agree that we should search out our cultural roots, provided that we recognize that, as Americans, our roots also come from all over the world, not just Western Europe.

The second claim, that only a study of Western civilization can teach a student how to think, is also partially true. Certainly, there is no better illustration of analytic thinking than Western civilization. Western science, Western technology, its organizational genius—all attest to the usefulness of breaking things down, whether to help us understand, or become efficient, or develop viable institutions. The university system, with its categorical divisions of schools, departments, subjects, credit hours, classroom periods rigidly set according to an organized plan, is the most familiar manifestation of the power of analytic thinking in the West.

But the literary critic M. H. Abrams reminds us about the dangers of analysis: "The endemic disease of analytical thinking," Abrams said, "is hardening of the categories" (1958, 34–35). Too many categories get hardened; institutions ossify; rules become intractable. The ailments of Western civilization, whether bureaucracies gone amok, or corporations that take abstractions for realities, or managers who see personnel and not people, are as much a legacy of analytic thinking as the triumphs of science and technology. I am not in favor of casting off the training that one receives in analytic thinking, in which the United States excels every other nation in the world, but I am against an excessive reliance on a Western perspective, excluding other points of view, regarding non-Western cultures as somehow benighted and underdeveloped. This closing off of the American mind into its Anglo-Saxon mind-set contradicts, ironically, one of the basic precepts in Western thinking, the belief that the educated mind is an open mind, that a democratic society is an open society. I do not need to quote Confucius and Buddha to refute Allan Bloom, E. D. Hirsch, and William Bennett and their insistence on the Judeo-Christian tradition as the only path to knowledge—John Stuart Mill will do. "It can do truth no service to blink [ignore] the fact," Mill wrote in *On Liberty*, "known to all who have the most ordinary acquaintance with literary history, that a large portion of the noblest and most valuable moral teaching has been the work, not only of men who did not know, but of men who knew and rejected, the Christian faith" (1947, 51). If Mill were alive today, he might be in favor of the very "ethnic studies" that the Blooms, Hirsches, and Bennetts of the world disparage. Mill celebrated a "plurality of paths"; he considered a "diversity of character and culture" to be a blessing, not a curse.

We cannot, of course, ignore the past, but most of us wouldn't want to repeat it. If we reflect on the past, especially the pre-modern past, we will notice that the key to the progressive development of Western tradition is its openness to new ideas, to other ways of thinking, its willingness not merely to modify but to revolutionize thinking. Is it any coincidence that in the modernized West of the last two hundred years there have been more revolutions—military, political, scientific, technological, ideological—than in all of human history? If one had to give a definition of *modern*, I would say that the term defines a period, a state of mind, in which revolutions are regarded as routine. Even hoary, well-established institutions like universities are *modern* in this sense: the modern university teaches disciplines that with some few exceptions, such as mathematics and classical studies, didn't exist two centuries ago. The other subjects were simply not recognized in the academy as viable subjects of study: psychology, chemistry, economics, French, Italian, biology, English literature, Germanic studies, Spanish, criminal justice, sociology, anthropology, computer science, journalism, geology, telecommunications, political science, religious studies, comparative literature, theater and drama. None of these courses of study were offered at the Sorbonne at the time of the French Revolution or at Oxford during the Victorian period. In fact, some of these subjects—computer science, for one—couldn't be found in university catalogs as recently as a generation ago.

There are some who ask if the liberal arts might not have become too liberal. They think that the liberal arts curriculum has become too unstructured, too unfocused. In a way, I agree: several courses of intellectual chop suey make for a grotesque meal, hardly digestible. But I would take issue with the implied use of the word *liberal* here, for *liberal* in the phrase *liberal arts* modifies not the *arts* but the person who is being educated. *Liberal arts* is an English translation of the Latin *artes liberales*, "the arts of free men." (The medieval period used the word *men* generically, but what was meant was "males": I also use the term generically, but I mean "men and women.") The phrase *liberal arts* in English confuses the modifier: it is a question of individuals who are free, not the arts.

To set people free, they must be educated, for ignorance is the greatest tyrant. As Plato said in his *Symposium*, "In this very point is ignorance distressing, that a person who is not enlightened or intelligent should be satisfied with himself. The man who does not feel himself defective has no desire for that whereof he feels no defect" (Lamb 1946, 183). But, when one asks if the liberal arts degree is too liberal, one must say no—for *liberal* means "free from narrow prejudice, open-minded." How can anyone be *too* free from narrow prejudice, *too* open-minded? There is no such thing as degrees of "open-mindedness"; one cannot be a little open-minded, just as one cannot be a little pregnant.

The point is that we need a liberal arts that will teach men and women how to be free. However, we must not confuse the student with the curriculum; we must avoid the imitative fallacy. Offering students total freedom of choice in what they want to learn does not teach freedom; the education of free men does not require anarchy in the classroom. I define the liberal arts as the disciplined and balanced contemplation of a comprehensive past that prepares the mind for *any* future—foreseen or unforeseen. The difference between technical training and the liberal arts is the difference between preparing for a profession and preparing for life. To prepare ourselves for freedom, we need discipline. Discipline is Paul Valéry writing poetry in strictly defined forms and describing the process as "dancing in chains." Discipline is Ty Cobb adding lead weights to his cleats when he trained for the baseball season so that he could run faster when it counted. Rigorous mental training requires a challenging and balanced program of education. We must be subjected to the stiffest tests in the classroom, precisely because there we have a chance to correct our mistakes and there the tests are usually fair; in life however, one doesn't always get a second chance, and the tests are, more often than not, unfair. The education of free men need not be an intellectual potpourri, a hodgepodge of "as you like it" courses. We are not like the animals, who are free but don't know it: our freedom must be earned; we must learn to be free; and we must know what to do with our freedom.

Liberty is another "L" word we don't hear much about nowadays. Perhaps it, too, has become a dirty word. There is a fear that there might be too much liberty, too much freedom of speech and thought. The American Civil Liberties Union (ACLU) has been attacked for protecting the civil liberties of too many people, including the Nazis in Skokie, Illinois, and all manner of social undesirables. During the 1988 election, the ACLU even protected the civil rights of some rather unpopular Republicans in a predominantly Democratic Brooklyn neighborhood. The ACLU is always busy. Censorship is alive and well in this country, in subtle and not so subtle forms. There are citizen groups that continue to demand the removal of *Catcher in the Rye* from libraries; there are campaigns to ban Anne Frank's *Diary* because she maintains that no one religion is superior to any other. Americans sometimes seem bent more on protecting liberty abroad than on nurturing it at home. Yes, *liberty* has become an "L" word nowadays, a shadow of its former self, a truncated husk of a word. Abbreviating *Liberty* makes a travesty of history. Will we speak of the "'L' Bell" in Philadelphia? And remember Patrick Henry's stirring words: "Give me 'L' or give me death!" America is in dire straits when *liberalism* and *liberty* are regarded as dirty words, when *liberalism* and *liberty* are abbreviated. The use of abbreviations is no warrant for abbreviated thinking.

There is fear and ignorance in the land. In 1981, a Chinese-

American named Vincent Chin was beaten to death with a baseball bat in Detroit by two unemployed auto workers who thought that he was Japanese: any "Oriental" was hateful because in their minds it was the Japanese who had put them out of work. In 1942, in the panic after Pearl Harbor, hundreds of thousands of Japanese-Americans, suspected of being Japanese agents, were uprooted from their homes and placed in internment camps in California and elsewhere. In 1987, Congress passed a bill providing reparations to the remaining survivors of these American concentration camps. However, the *Terre Haute Tribune-Star* published a letter to the editor *protesting* the bill: why should we pay *them*, the letter said, when the Japanese won't pay our remaining survivors of *their* concentration camps. The letter-writer did not know, and the *Tribune-Star*—to its everlasting shame—failed to point out, that sixty thousand of those incarcerated in Manzanar and other camps during the Second World War were not prisoners of war: *they were American citizens!* We cannot speak of a free press when that press allows ignorance to proclaim itself unchecked; no press is free that is itself ignorant. Florida and California, the two states with the largest Latino/Latina populations, have passed referendums to make English the official language: need one add that the referendums were publicized in English and the ballot provided only in English. The propaganda for English as the official language cites instance after instance where Americans are ignorant of English. "It's frightening," the promotional letter says. My own primary language is English, and English is the language I know best. I even teach freshman composition. But I will not support the exclusive use of English in this country. Indeed, I see in the English-only movement the seeds of racism. Whites in Florida and California are being outnumbered by Asians and Latinos/Latinas. Demographers all agree that whites will be in the minority in this country by the year 2000. What kind of democracy is it that advocates rule of the majority only when that majority is white, only when that majority speaks English?

During the 1988 election campaign, I saw a bumper sticker that read, "There are Americans, and then there are liberals." Even those educated in a curriculum that taught the core of Western tradition would recall that American "liberals" include: Thomas Jefferson, Abraham Lincoln, Franklin Delano Roosevelt, and John Fitzgerald Kennedy. I have been proud to be an American, but there are definitions of *American* in some quarters of which I want no part. Groucho Marx once said that he would not join any club that would admit him as a member. If not being a liberal is all that it takes to be an American, then I would rather not be a member of this club called America.

There is a growing "know-nothing" movement in this country, a "shoot first and ask questions later" mentality that is a powerful blend of fear, hate, and ignorance—and the greatest threat to liberty. Before the increasing complexity of modern life, there is a retreat into orthodoxy and dogma. There are large segments of the country who would rather not think and be right than think and be wrong. "Truth gains more," to quote Mill again, "even by the errors of one who with due study and preparation, thinks for himself, than by the true opinions of those who only hold them because they do not suffer to think" (1947, 33). This abnegation of responsibility, this unwillingness to protect the most essential liberty, liberty of thought, is a threat to true democracy. John Milton, that most God-loving author of *Paradise Lost*, perhaps liberty's greatest champion, wrote in *Areopagitica*, "Give me the liberty to know, to utter, and to argue freely according to conscience, above all liberties" (1959, 2:560).

Unthinking inaction is also an erosion of democracy. 50.1 percent of the eligible voters voted in the 1988 election, 55.2 percent in 1992, which means that nearly half those with the right to vote in this country don't. (In 1992, there were, according to the 1993 census figures, 189 million eligible voters; 44.8 percent, or nearly eighty-five million U.S. citizens, failed to vote in the last presidential election.) The refusal, as much out of fear as out of ignorance, to wrestle with difficult social and ethical problems, the impatience with anything complicated, the unwillingness to see more than one side of an issue—these are as much threats to our system of democracy as any threat, military or economic, from abroad. If one compares the federal expenditures on defense and on education, one can hardly avoid the conclusion that we may fast be becoming the most expensively protected nation of "know-nothings" in the world. Fortunately, the fall of the Iron Curtain has reduced the pressure for ever-increasing defense spending; the question now is whether one will be wise enough to recognize that a nation's greatest defense is in a population that is well educated—just as it is, to recall Thomas Jefferson, democracy's surest guarantee.

No one would deny that life in the twentieth century is more complex than it was in Jefferson's time. Thoughtful people can recognize the validity of both sides of an issue, and there doesn't always seem to be a clear-cut answer to every question. However, politicians who seek votes—as well as talk show hosts who seek audiences—will exploit our intellectual laziness and offer simplistic answers. They remove our frustrations at the increasing complexities that we face and reassure us, falsely, that the problem does not require any further thought. One is offered verities, things unquestioned and unarguable, instead of truth, that which must always be questioned and argued, tempered in the fire of debate. And all this in the name of an Americanism that does not know its own history. Many Americans are, unfortunately, familiar with Confucius only as the butt of countless popular jokes that begin with "Confucius say. . . ." But, twenty-five hundred years ago, Confucius said, "If a State is governed by the principles of reason, poverty and misery are subjects of shame;

if a state is *not* governed by the principles of reason, riches and honors are the subjects of shame" (*Analects*, 8:13). Despite its foreign source, this quote is woven into the fabric of the American tradition because it is cited in one of the classics of American literature: Henry David Thoreau's *Civil Disobedience*. I leave it to you to determine whether "poverty and misery" or "riches and honors" are the subjects of shame in our time. The obscene wealth of junk bond manipulators, savings-and-loan embezzlers, as well as the equally obscene presence of the multitudes of the homeless on our city streets, may suggest that one doesn't have to look far for subjects of shame.

The essence of a love for truth is the courage to be wrong, rather than a smugness about being right. Science is not a perfect instance of infallibility; it is not a basic core of received truth. It is, if anything, a dynamic tradition of trial and error, of experiment and theory, of assertion and correction. Science is a self-correcting computer. Every great scientist, from Tycho Brahe to Galileo to Newton to Einstein, has been subsequently proved wrong in one respect or another. In 1965, when asked why it was taking him so long to edit the Einstein papers (Einstein had died ten years before), J. Robert Oppenheimer reported that Einstein made a number of mistakes that needed to be corrected. And then, Oppenheimer added, with admiration, "But what mistakes!" In physics, no one today finds adequate the model of an atom as a solar system, with electrons revolving around a nucleus of protons and neutron, yet it was precisely with this model that Ernest Rutherford won the Nobel Prize in 1915. Even traditional notions of reason have been overthrown in the last decade or so. What was regarded as anathema to an orderly understanding of the universe, chaos, is now regarded as the beginnings of a new science: the science of chaos affects almost everything, from our ability to predict the weather, to the behavior of the economy, to an understanding of biological processes. This revolution is not so much against reason, for the new chaos theorists are not mad, but against static and rigid notions of reason. These thinkers advocate a dynamic, constantly expanding base of reason.

Nothing could be more unreasonable than to see reason as a fixed doxology that deflects rather than reflects thought. If we have not discovered all there is to discover, if we have not lost our courage to explore, we will develop a *creative* "know-nothing" attitude, where the recognition of our own ignorance and provinciality inspires more speculative inquiry, encourages more rather than less liberal thinking. There is this difference between a negative and a positive "know-nothing" attitude: one says, "I know nothing, and that's good enough for me"; the other says: "What I know is nothing, and what I know is not nearly enough."

Knowledge liberates, we are told; the truth will set you free. But we must be careful, for those of us who have acquired a little learning must recognize that it's a dangerous thing to become complacent about what we have learned. Complacent knowledge can become a prison, self-satisfied knowledge a curse. We cannot allow knowledge to instill a false sense of superiority; we must avoid the arrogance of those who inflate the value of what they know by deflating the value of what they don't know. We cannot emulate the attitude depicted in a rather scurrilous ditty about Benjamin Jowett, the great classical scholar, who was master of Balliol College, Oxford, in the last thirty years of the nineteenth century. "I am Benjamin Jowett," the ditty runs, "I'm master of Balliol College":

> *I know just about everything,*
> *And what I don't know isn't knowledge.*

We cannot allow knowledge—especially the knowledge that we acquired in college—to imprison us in arrogance; we cannot let what we *do* know prevent us from learning what we *don't* know. I have never liked the phrase *educated person*, because it suggests that the process of learning is over once the course of study is finished: a truly educated person never stops learning. Learning becomes a habit, an obsession. People who see being educated just in terms of achievement do not understand that, unless one has opened all doors to knowledge, one has not been well and truly educated. These doors both admit the light from outside and permit the light to shine from within. "The light by which we see in this world," Emerson tells us, "comes out from the soul of the observer" (1904, 296). Arrogance hoards knowledge; humility seeks it; wisdom shares it. Education opens doors; it does not close them.

A liberal education is not the road to El Dorado, a utopia of unthinking joy and rapture. It is arduous because it forces us to develop ourselves only by respecting others; it is perilous because it exposes us to our own errors and the pitfalls of false reason; and it is lonely because it is Robert Frost's road "less traveled by." "Success" will beckon us from this road, and we will be tempted to pursue it at any cost (which is why William James astutely characterized success as "the bitch-goddess"). We will need to be strong, particularly when profits seem more attractive than principle, when status stands for more than self-respect, when interest means more than integrity. J. R. Ewing of "Dallas," the incorrigible scoundrel of prime time soap opera, is the epitome of a shallow success. How does J. R. explain his success? "Without integrity," he quips, "it's a piece of cake!" Smart people who are unscrupulous will always be able to wangle their way to success. The question is not whether you will be a success. The question is what kind of success are you going to be. Do you have what it takes truly to succeed—even when you know that it won't be "a piece of cake"? When success and integrity are at odds, which will you prefer? As the line from the country and western song goes, "If you don't stand for something, you'll fall for anything."

The true patriot in America sees a diverse and pluralistic America; the true patriot does not mask her own self-interests under the shibboleths of a recited pledge of allegiance. Freedom *of* religion in America also means freedom *from* religion: one is not obliged to believe in God at all. The undercurrents of fear have never been stronger in this country, and appeals to fear are now more persuasive than appeals to reason. The appeal to patriotism, out of hatred toward the foreign rather than love for one's own country, underlies a new wave of isolationism, a fortress mentality, a virulent strain of cultural racism. For some Americans, there is only one kind of true red-blooded American: and that kind is not black, or Asian, or Latino/Latina, not even Native American.

But patriotism—"the last refuge of the scoundrel," Dr. Johnson reminds us—is no excuse. True patriotism is compassionate toward one's countrymen; true patriotism never forgets the ideals on which the country was founded.

Whatever threats to national security exist today, they could not have been greater than in 1941. Vulnerable from the east and from the west; we were being threatened by Germany in the Atlantic, Japan in the Pacific. In that year, Hollywood produced one of the most patriotic films ever made, *Casablanca*. It not only succeeded in stirring up national fervor but also managed to become an American classic. But the patriotism in *Casablanca* never loses sight of what it is to be truly American, what distinguishes this country from all others. We all remember Rick's café, where most of the action takes place, perhaps the most famous "gin-joint in all the world." Rick's café attracted the most motley collection of gamblers, spies, Resistance fighters, refugees, Russians, Bulgarians, Arabs, Blacks, corrupt French officials, beautiful women, and, yes, even Nazis! Yet we must not forget the full name of this saloon: "Rick's Café Americain." Rick Blaine reminds me of the American Civil Liberties Union and of America: his Café Americain admitted everyone and anyone, provided that there was no violence. The Café Americain was a place for dreamers and schemers, for newlyweds and for old couples, for the cynic and the romantic, for the honest and the corrupt. It didn't matter who you were or what you believed in; it was a place where the only battle waged was a singing duel and the weapons used were national anthems; it was a place where the roulette table was rigged, sometimes even in favor of young idealists and romantics.

I think of the end of that movie and of the fresh-faced Ingrid Bergman, with her broad-brimmed hat casting the most intriguing shadow across her brow, a symbol of beauty and hope, her eyes glistening, about to step on the plane to Lisbon and to freedom. Young people are about to "take off," each on a different plane to Lisbon. And, taking the prerogative of every moviegoer to assume a role of choice, let me say in the voice of Paul Henreid as Victor Laszlo, "I hope you will fight the good fight. I hope you will fight for liberty, liberalism, and the liberal arts. Vive le Café Americain!"

But, in the end, one can't resist assuming Humphrey Bogart's voice, so, in that voice, I'd like to say to the young people of this world what Humphrey Bogart says twice to the radiant, fresh-faced Ingrid Bergman in the film, words that are inevitable in the movies but just a little preposterous in real life:

"Here's looking at you, kid!"

CHAPTER SEVEN

The Complexities of Complexion:
The Myths of Skin Color

O formose puer, nimium ne crede colori
(O handsome lad, don't trust too much in your complexion).   VIRGIL

Among the unfortunate consequences of any struggle for cultural identity is that it unhelpfully polarizes race relations between, literally, white and black. When the immigrants from Africa and their descendants were, in Ralph Ellison's memorable image, "invisible"—in a culture that only recognized an all-American white—their identity could not be reclaimed except in dramatic black-against-white contrasts. In the forty years or more since *Brown v. Board of Education*, when the notion of "separate but equal" was struck down and the Supreme Court decided that equal opportunity was meaningless without racial integration, the terms *white* and *black* have become so monolithic that in the popular imagination races are seen as clearly as white against black or black against white. Certainly this provides a convenient image that is easily exploited by the media and just as easily manipulated by demagogues. These shortcuts—like abbreviations—have a way of establishing their own reality; in time, people begin to think of them as more real than the reality they were supposed to represent. The whole notion of black and white conflicts with any coherent understanding of, or appreciation for, color. Movies acquired Technicolor half a century ago, color television has been generally available for the last two decades, even old black and white movies have been—dubiously—"colorized," yet our minds are still in the era of black-and-white. The irony in all this is that neither white nor black is a color. In terms of optics, black is the absence of color, and white is the presence of all the colors. As a physicist friend said to me, with the resonance of what he was saying going beyond physics, "White has no wave length of its own."

There is talk nowadays of "people of color"—thereby including Latinos/Latinas (browns), Native Americans (reds), and Asian-Americans (yellows). Yet even a consideration of "people of color" exaggerates and confuses the issue. We are, after all, talking about individuals, not color-coded merchandise. These color labels are like machine-readable UPC's, universal "people" codes: they provide instantaneous inventory control. Once you register the color, then you can catalog ethnic profiles, demographics, earning power, IQ, annual income, voting patterns, etc. In all this ethnic consciousness, it is, ironically, the individual who gets lost in the kaleidoscope.

First of all, we must dispel the myth that color codes—or their ultimate oversimplification in white and black—are accurate, or even convenient, markers of race. "Orientals" are no more "yellow" than some other races:[1] they do not have a higher incidence of jaundice than Caucasians, nor is their skin pigmentation markedly different from that of Europeans: some indeed are as brown as Melanesians or East Indians, others as pale as Scandinavians. Nor are the other color characterizations of race very accurate:

---

1. Although anyone sensitive to language cannot help but register the overtones of characterizing Orientals as *yellow*, similar racist implications were inherent in such labels as *Mongoloid* and *Mongolism* to indicate mental deficiency: the more scientific term in use today is *Down syndrome*.

the "red Indian," anthropologists claim with increasing certainty, is descended from the original Asiatic migrants who came to North America over the land bridge that existed where the Bering Strait is now:[2] if we follow the racial color code, they might be thought of as "off-yellow." (There is also some evidence for transoceanic migrants from Asia and Melanesia.) The cranial resemblance of some Native Americans to Asians may be seen even today.[3] *Black* imprecisely covers pigmentation that ranges all the way from pitch black to off-white: there are "blacks" who are chocolate colored ("Chocolate Thunder") and "blacks" whose skin color is tan ("Mocha Maid") as well as "blacks" whose complexion is as "white" at that of a "white." And if *brown* is to designate the normative Latino/Latina, what about the skin color of Arab-Americans and Indian-Americans; what "color" is left to designate them as different from the other ethnics?

Our terminology often obscures or neglects real issues. For example, isn't there a difference, say, between someone who comes to the United States from Japan and becomes a U.S. citizen and someone who is the offspring of a Japanese and an American parent? Yet both these are designated *Japanese-Americans*. In the one case, the hyphen represents acculturation, in the second case a mixed biological inheritance. In a poll conducted by *Time* magazine ("The New Face of America" 1993, 14), it was estimated that nearly two-thirds of Japanese-Americans (U.S. citizens who are ethnically Japanese) marry non-Japanese Americans. How would we differentiate these biracial offspring from their one bicultural Japanese-American parent? Do we call them Japanese-American-Americans?

As for white, if truth be told, many white Americans appear

---

2. Some claim that the migration over the land bridge went the other way, from the Americas to Asia.

3. There are also broad cultural similarities, including ancestor-worship, reverence for the land, strong patriarchal social structure, and respect for elders.

to have skin that is flush pink (and not only when they've had too much to drink). In the psycholinguistics of language use, one need not wonder why *pink* was not more usable than *white* as a descriptor of race. And what is it that habituates us to see hair that shades from yellow to near-white as blonde and hair that shades from brown to black as brunette? In fact, the shades of skin color among Caucasians occupy almost as wide a spectrum as the color of other races—from the leathery brown of some Floridians to the ghostly pallor of some Minnesotans.

With all these variations within groups labeled by one color code, it's a wonder one notices differences between groups at all; and if one does, it's certainly not always on the basis of color. Still, we distinguish between a very light-skinned black and a very tanned Caucasian with no trouble, but it is clearly not on the basis of skin color exclusively. These are ocular confusions that our "cultured" eye filters out easily: they are oversimplified by the myths of color.

There is, of course, a color prejudice (not only in the United States) for and against light-skinned people of African descent, but, were mere skin pigmentation a reliable index of our regard for another, then suntans would hardly be fashionable among those with pale skins. In the designation of colors for different races, there is both more and less than meets the eye. We make too much of color, and too little. Some light-skinned African-Americans may be suspected of "passing for white," but few Caucasians, no matter how tanned, are ever accused of "passing for black."⁴ Blacks today find white actors using "blackface"

4. One of those who did was John Howard Griffin, whose experiences were recorded in his landmark book, *Black like Me* (1961). I find it interesting that, while there are derogatory terms for ethnics who try to pass for white—*Oreos* (black on the outside, white on the inside) for Uncle Toms, *bananas* (yellow on the outside, white on the inside) for Asian-Americans—there appear to be no derogatory image for whites passing for blacks, perhaps because, given the social victimization of blacks, so few whites would want to pass for black. There are, however, the counterinstances,

offensive, yet no white is offended by anyone using "whiteface." And, if "lily white" is the ultimate ideal, why aren't albinos prized beyond all others? Color is a convenient form of oversimplification that subsumes other prejudices. But color designations are themselves so mixed up that they cannot be categorically precise.[5] Clearly, color in and of itself is not a reliable index, not even for the purposes of racial discrimination.

There is a myth about the color white that is speciously regarded as universal in some quarters. White connotes purity and perfection, unsullied virtue, virginity (as in white wedding gowns), wholesomeness (as in milk); it is also regarded as the symbol of cleanliness. In American culture, these images have become so conventionalized that the word *white* is no longer a neutral marker. Yet not all white is necessarily good and wholesome (remember Moby Dick?), nor is any other color—including black, brown, yellow, or red—necessarily less healthy. Indeed, in Eastern cultures, white is variously symbolic of death, corruption, and evil. In traditional Chinese drama, the actor who wears the white mask is the villain, and the one who wears the black is often the hero. There are generic as well as cultural reinforcements for this privileging of white over black.

The cognate contrasts to white and black are light and dark. And, as the progress of Western civilization has advanced, from the Renaissance (which ended the Dark Ages) to the Enlighten-

especially in music, when white singers might be complimented for singing with "soul." Some consider Elvis Presley and Buddy Holly before him to be white singers who, at least on occasion, sang like blacks. Many current white performers of rock music imitate black models.

5. The scientific study of color itself is a complex problem: as one scholar has written, "The assignment of colors to objects . . . on the basis of their physical light-transforming properties proves to be a very complicated matter. An object turns out to have a transmission color, a reflection color, an interference color, etc., no two necessarily the same, and each color is a function of detection angle as well as of the spectrum of the incident light" (Hardin 1988, 6–7).

ment, light has been preferred over dark, day over night. Place names have tended to enshrine implicit prejudices: where geography is theoretically objective, geographic names are anything but neutral. Africa was known for centuries as "the Dark Continent," defining that territory in terms of the West's ignorance of it. Presumably, Africa was not dark to the local Africans, and they might have been puzzled that the land in which they lived would be called *dark* by anyone. One can only speculate on the extreme ethnocentricity of labeling something by how little one understood it. The notion of *dark* evoked not just a "benighted" culture but one whose very blackness suggested impenetrable evil. These associations of mystery, of blackness, and of evil were, of course, brilliantly exploited by Conrad in his *Heart of Darkness*—which reveals much more about Eurocentric paranoia than it does about the heart of Africa.

The psychology of color, as reflected in language and culture, has as much to do with the complexities of prejudice as with prejudices about complexion. In the minds of many, white is associated with good and black with evil. When we use *white* and *black* as racial markers, they are far from the neutral labels that we think we're using: there is at least a subliminal, certainly a subconscious meaning being conveyed through the cultural associations of black and white. No one characterized as *black-hearted* is likely to be admired—although the language does not afford its counterpart, someone who is *white-hearted*. The "black is beautiful" movement of the 1960s may have mitigated some of these color prejudices. Yet race conflicts will never be resolved until we dispel the prejudicial mind-set of seeing things and people in terms of white and black, until we recognize the prejudicial and the stereotypical effect of color designations.

Prejudice is an attitude that reflects a presumptive and presumptuous knowledge about an individual or a situation based— rightly or wrongly—on preconceived ideas. The operative effect of prejudice, even when it is successfully withstood, is that the victim of prejudice is deprived of a natural expression of her own identity. Prejudice is, therefore, inherent in any racial label because none of us acts "white," "black," "brown," "red," or "yellow": within a social, cultural, historical, and economic matrix, each of us acts as an individual.

There is no simple answer to the question how to treat blacks, or Asian-Americans, or Latinos/Latinas, or Native Americans. The hard work of personal relations cannot be codified. Among whites, there are pseudoliberals who think that they are enlightened because they know how to deal with different ethnic groups: "save face" with "Orientals"; assume "machismo" with Latinos and Latinas; walk loose and talk jive with blacks. But these "accommodations" are only marginally better than outright bigotry because they suffer from the same erroneous premise: that members of a group are conformist clones of each other—what is true for one is assumed to be true for all members of the group.[6]

Color designations of race are a disservice for another reason: not only do they misrepresent individual members of ethnic groups, they fail to represent individuals who are descended from more than one ethnic or racial group, who are mixed-race offspring, hereditarily neither one "color" nor another but both—

6. In March 1992, there was a flap in the sports pages about a photograph that exploitative newsgatherers published, showing the Indiana University basketball coach, who is white, "whipping" a black player with a towel. This elicited knee-jerk reactions against Bobby Knight's bad taste, which, of course, ignored the fact that the jest was the inspiration of the players themselves: nor did the accusations of racial bias in his abuse take into account that Knight took a towel to white players as well (the photographs of those encounters were, presumably, thought unworthy of publication). White liberals wanted the coach to be reprimanded, taking surrogate offense for the black community. Some blacks in Bloomington, Indiana, *were* offended, but other blacks, even some very prominent blacks, were not. The point about this knee-jerk brand of liberalism is that liberalism, above all, cannot be without a sense of self-irony, or else it begins to resemble fascism, which is notoriously humorless.

or more. According to the *New York Times* (8 June 1991), quoting Albert Woolbright, a sociologist at the National Center for Health Statistics, "Births to black-and-white couples more than quintupled from 1968 (9,600) to 1988 (51,000)"—as contrasted with a general 12 percent growth in the overall population. According to the same report, more than half the Asian-Americans in the United States intermarry with non-Asians, usually with whites. There is a growing segment of the population that will be difficult if not impossible to "color code." And, if truth be known, there probably has always been a significant proportion of the population of "mixed blood," which over time and through the generations has evolved into an indistinct and undefinable meld of races. In times past, these mixed-race offspring might have been an embarrassment to the families of either parent, or sometimes of both, but the nature of American life as well as human nature will preclude the genetic segregation of ethnic identities. There are multi-ethnic interracial student coalitions springing up on college campuses for multiracial individuals who refuse to "opt" for one race or another in establishing their identity. We can argue about the image of America shifting from the melting pot to a mosaic, but, for individuals who are multiracial, the metaphors are no longer abstract: culturally, they resemble a melting pot, but, genetically, they resemble a mosaic.

Comprehensive surveys of voting patterns and of economic profiles blithely ignore these multiethnic individuals. There is a compulsion, by sociologists and poll takers, to compartmentalize everyone so as more easily to fit preconceived categories.

Our rhetoric has lagged behind our reality. The colors that we use, the ethnic designations that have hardened into conventional categories, do not fit a significant proportion of the population. The consequences of modern-day travel, of the mobility of Americans within the United States and throughout the world, will mean that fewer and fewer Americans will marry "their own kind," fewer and fewer will marry their "high school sweet-hearts." If Americans, on the average, are marrying later in life, then the chances of their marrying people of recent rather than long-standing acquaintance will increase. The chances of these prospective spouses being from cultures other than the one in which they were raised are also enhanced. There will come a time when color designations of race and ethnicity will be more cumbersome to use than they're worth. It may turn out that these terms were not very helpful in the first place, that they exacerbated the very problems that they were invented to solve. Our language must change with the changing reality if we are to communicate effectively with each other in confronting new realities. The very form of survey questionnaires is prejudicial: when one does not fit in the category of either Caucasian, Asian, Latino/Latina, African, or Arab, one must mark "Other," either because one belongs to a category not significant enough for inclusion or because one belongs in more than one category. There is a value judgment being made between "mainstream" minorities and "backwater" minorities. In time, however, more and more people will find themselves in the "Other" category.[7]

The momentum of history will be toward what used to be condemned by most cultures: history will move more toward miscegenation than ever before. But one would be wrong to conceive of miscegenation as a modern phenomenon. Many of

---

7. It is ironic that, in a country so jealous of individual privacy, there should be a general assumption that a person's ethnicity is part of the public's right to know. My wife was once asked over the phone by a telemarketing salesman posing as a poll taker to answer a few questions. When she was asked about her ethnic background, she replied, quietly, that she considered the question offensive and an intrusion of privacy—whereupon the telemarketer told my wife that he found *her* offensive (in making it difficult, I suppose, for him to make a living at her expense). Some people just do not realize that the telephone (not to say the media) does not give universal rights of access: we let strangers into our homes through the telephone and the media that we would not think of admitting if they came to our front door.

the "races" designated as distinct from others are themselves racial composites. Take the Chinese, for example. There are Turkic, Manchurian, Min, and Tungusic strains in the Chinese people. Monolithic as it might appear to outsiders, even China is an interracial and intercultural country. Surely the successive dominations of the Eurasian land mass—by the Greeks, the Romans, the Huns, the Mongols, and the Turks—all left their genetic imprint on the local populations. Even Englishmen are composites of different ethnic and racial stocks: Angles, Saxons, Normans, Celts, Danes. The ethnic and racial mixtures of history are too often forgotten in the ideology of a monolithic culture and a hegemonic nationalism. A retroactive purity is imputed to ancestors by descendants who, ironically, don't know their own heritage, much less their genealogy. But only the most isolated tribes are ethnically and racially "pure." The intermixture of races, in the perspective of history, is more the norm than the exception. Only cultural reactionaries and rabid nationalists, more wedded to their own notions of "purity" than to the realities of the past, insist on denying what they find ideologically repugnant.

In an often antiseptic modernist culture, where deadly viruses and contaminations and pollutions have inured us to a notion of "purity" as being essential to health, there is a strong prejudice against "mixtures" and "impurities." But evolution tells us that, without the wayward, "impure," mutant genetic strains, there would have been no "descent of man" or any "ascent of man." The irony is that what is "preserved" soon becomes extinct. Survival may lie precisely in the flexibility and adaptability of mutant, mulatto, hybrid strains. It is the impurity of a mote of dust around which the beauty of the snowflake collects. "Emerald and ruby," writes C. L. Hardin, "owe their color to the very same impurity, chromium" (1988, 5). Diversity may be a principle in the survival of the species. Those who wish to preserve a static culture unwittingly doom it to extinction. The only things that don't change gather dust in a museum or are pickled—preserved—in formaldehyde. Nothing that has life, that is capable of change, can be considered absolutely pure.

The recognition of complexities in our thoughts about race and skin color should not come as a surprise. We are, after all, each of us, insistent on our own uniqueness, our own identity as complex individuals. Why should we think of groups of individuals as being less complex than a single individual? America was predicated on a complex unity: thirteen states, each autonomous and different, forming a union. We have managed a model of federal authority and states rights that has held together for two hundred years. There are now fifty states, and the federal union is as strong as it has ever been. We have proved that it is possible to preserve a union without erasing local and regional identities. Political pluralism presupposes cultural and racial pluralism. One entails the other. Those who advocate the importance of states rights in a federal context should have no difficulty comprehending the importance of ethnic identities within a unified population of Americans. Paradoxically, we will be more at one the more each of us is different from each other. The only pluralism that cannot survive is the pluralism of two, of antinomian opposites, of black against white, of North against South.

I came across an instructive fable in a travel magazine that illustrates the point:

> Three men stood at the riverbank with their guru. The river was full of snapping crocodiles. One man crossed, calling out, "Rama, Rama, Rama." And the crocodiles cleared a path for him. The second man crossed, calling, "Allah, Allah, Allah," and the crocodiles parted and cleared a path for him. The third man crossed, calling, "Buddha, Buddha, Buddha." And the crocodiles cleared a path for him. And the guru said,

"Hmmm, what strong words, what strong magic." So he crossed, calling, "Rama-Allah-Buddha"—and the crocodiles immediately devoured him. That night each of the three men who had safely crossed the river had a dream: "You saw what happened to your guru. I am Rama. I am Allah. I am Buddha. But I am not Rama-Allah-Buddha. You must believe in one. I am One." (adapted from *Condé Nast Traveler*, June 1993, 160)

The United States is one; it is not Alabama – Alaska – Arizona – Arkansas – California – Colorado – Connecticut – Delaware – Florida – Georgia – Hawaii – Idaho – Illinois – Indiana – Iowa – Kansas – Kentucky – Louisiana – Maine – Maryland – Massachusetts – Michigan – Minnesota – Mississippi – Missouri – Montana – Nebraska – Nevada – New Hampshire – New Jersey – New Mexico – New York – North Carolina – North Dakota – Ohio – Oklahoma – Oregon – Pennsylvania – Rhode Island – South Carolina – South Dakota – Tennessee – Texas – Utah – Vermont – Virginia – Washington – West Virginia – Wisconsin – Wyoming, plus Puerto Rico – Virgin Islands – the District of Columbia – Guam.

The question is whether the United States of America is going to be a country of principle, regardless of shifts in demographics, or a country with a mandated cultural and racial profile, with no regard for principle. Are the Americans of the future going to be determined by race or skin color or by the principles that they share?

CHAPTER EIGHT

Blind to Color, Deaf to Accent: Invisible and Inaudible Immigrants

> Prejudices are what fools use for reason.
> VOLTAIRE, *Poème sur la vie naturelle*

Immigrant. It's funny how much *immigrant* sounds like *ignorant*. People with status who come to the United States from abroad are called *émigrés* or *exiles*. "Boat people" are "immigrants"; the passengers of the Mayflower are "exiles," yet they were the original "boat people." Why are the boat people of the seventeenth century hallowed in American memory and the boat people of the twentieth century, who risk hazards no less perilous, whose thirst for freedom is no less noble, the objects of American hostility?

One reason for the difference relates to the level of education. The Mayflower passengers were religious dissidents who were, nevertheless, educated. Passage on the Mayflower reflected not only wealth but culture. Another reason is race. The word *immigrant* becomes negative the more the proportion of immigrant populations becomes nonwhite. Nowadays, when 90 percent of all legal immigrants are nonwhite, the word *immigrant* has become almost pejorative.

Perceptions are, for better or worse, important in today's personal interactions ("Image is everything," the ad claims), but their complexities are not often explored. For example, are we more influenced by sight or sound or smell? (I leave aside taste and touch as senses experienced only in intimate contact, which is often precluded by off-putting behaviors involving the other three senses.) Is it more disadvantageous to look like an immigrant or to sound like an immigrant?

There are what I call *presumed invisibilities*, many tied to erroneous notions of color, that are part of the problem. These presumed invisibilities elicit misunderstanding, hostility, resentment, and humor. The anecdotes that follow serve to undercut any notion that an American can be identified accurately by eye or ear, by the color of her skin or the sound of his voice. That shouldn't be surprising because no one denies that America is an idea, not a race, that it is a way of life, not an ideology, and that at the base of what defines this country is a tolerance of many points of view, an acceptance of many religious faiths, and a receptivity to many cultures. If this is so, and one reads it in the Declaration of Independence as well as the Constitution, why does one still hear boasts about "a dominant culture" and people insisting that that dominant culture continue to be white Anglo-Saxon Protestant? If South Africa has been, until recent developments, the country of white minority rule, then the United States has been the country of white majority rule. But majorities are not irrevocably fixed: they can change over time. In Florida and California, they are already changing.

Years ago, when I worked in a publishing house on Park Avenue, I related an incident to a young, blonde, female colleague of Scandinavian descent. Our office was on the eighth floor, and in the bank of elevators that divided up the access to the skyscraper, one bank of elevators covered floors 2–9. The ninth floor was occupied by the offices of the Mitsubishi Incorporated (in the 1960s, Japanese companies were not as common in New York City as they are today). I had just come back from lunch at a neighborhood Japanese restaurant, and, as it happened, there were some Japanese businessmen who left the restaurant the same time I did. I walked back to my office building, and they came in the same direction. I went toward the bank of elevators that went from 2 to 9, and they came along. When the elevator arrived, I went in, and they came in as well. I pressed the button for the eighth floor, and, when the doors opened, I exited. Although my facial features are clearly Chinese and I stand almost six feet tall, the Mitsubishi employees must have assumed, reinforced by the coincidence of my choosing the same restaurant, the same office building, and the same bank of elevators, that I, too, worked for Mitsubishi. When I got out at the eighth floor, the contingent from Mitsubishi exited as well. Then, as the elevator door closed and they noticed the unfamiliar surroundings, there was general consternation and a volley of "O desuka ne!" all around. I thought this episode amusing enough, but my female colleague responded with an incident of her own. The story that she told illustrates what I mean by *presumed invisibilities*, but it adds a twist, since the gist of the story hinges on her being decidedly visible to the eye and on her presumed invisibility in Japanese.

My blonde colleague was, even at a young age, extremely accomplished: among her achievements was a command of Japanese. The incident that she related was a cognate of mine, but with a different ending. She, too, had gone to the Japanese restaurant. She, too, came out of the restaurant just about the time a group of Japanese businessmen came out. She, too, was followed by the Japanese back to the same building, the same bank of elevators, the same elevator. In the elevator, she found herself the only Caucasian among Japanese men and conspicuously taller than they. All the way from the first to the eighth floor, the Japanese spoke among themselves in Japanese, appraising her physical attractions. When I reconstruct her story in my mind, I cannot help but think of my friend, whose complexion was fair and who was prone to blushing, turning pink as the elevator ascended from the ground floor to the eighth floor. When she exited at the eighth floor, predictably, no one followed her. As soon as she stepped off, my friend turned around facing the elevator full of Japanese men and, bowing deeply, said *in fluent Japanese* how honored she was by their compliments. The elevator door, as if on cue, closed, leaving the Japanese in some consternation.

What interests me about this incident is that both visibility and invisibility were at work. My colleague was certainly conspicuously visible to the Japanese. Yet, when they spoke in their native language, assuming plausibly that she could not understand their language, they were treating her as one who did not know what they were saying: in effect, she was treated as if she were not there. That's why one feels so viscerally excluded when one cannot converse in the language being spoken: it's as if one doesn't exist, as if one were invisible. My friend felt invisible overhearing a conversation about her. The rub in this case was that she *did* know the language. But, because of her fair skin pigmentation, she was presumed invisible in Japanese.

A pendant incident happened to me some years later. I was being interviewed on a live television talk show in Indianapolis on the question of racism. In the same segment, there was to be an interview with a elderly gentleman who had published the *Daily Macedonian* in Fort Wayne, Indiana, for half a century and who had just written a book about his early immigrant experiences. Even after fifty years, he spoke with a thick Macedonian accent. There was a third guest. Just what relevance his expertise had to the subjects of the other two interviews—race and the immigrant experience—was not altogether obvious to me. He was a professor of criminology at a small Midwestern college whose specialty was serial murderers. This academic was professorial, with thinning blonde hair, Mr. Peepers glasses, and a scholarly, somewhat timorous demeanor.

The expert on serial murders was interviewed first, myself second, and the former publisher of the *Daily Macedonian* last. In my segment, I made the point that I was a "visible immigrant." My face revealed my ancestral origins whereas many immigrants or descendants of immigrants were invisible. Their immigrant origins were not manifest in the way they looked (this included the interviewer, an attractive blonde who had told me prior to the live interview that her grandfather was Macedonian, indeed a friend of the Macedonian-American publisher). In other words, although we, the interviewer and I, were both American citizens, being a "visible immigrant" I was regarded as more foreign than she was. It was only when I stepped down from the klieg lights and chatted with the professor of criminology that I received an unexpected affirmation of my theory of invisibility. The professor of criminology confided in me that he was more "foreign" than I was. Here he was, not looking or sounding foreign, claiming that he *was* foreign. "I'm a Canadian," he said, "and I'm here on a green card." Our criminologist friend was an "invisible foreigner."

The ironies of this encounter were instructive. The two people who looked or sounded "foreign" weren't, and the person who did not look or sound "foreign" was. My Macedonian-American friend and I were not obvious Americans but manifest immigrants or manifestly descended from immigrants (he was betrayed by accent, I by race), whereas our criminologist friend was an invisible and inaudible foreigner, who could and did pass for an American. Nor is he alone: many prominent figures in American life are Canadians: some of them immigrated from Canada to be sure, but others continue to live in the United States with Canadian citizenship and are, regardless of appearances, not American. Mary Pickford, "America's Sweetheart," came from Toronto. The economist John Kenneth Galbraith is Canadian. Such institutions of American pop culture as Peter Jennings, Art Linkletter, Mort Sahl, Rich Little, Dan Akroyd, and Lorne Michaels (director of "Saturday Night Live") all came from Canada. (*New York Times*, 27 June 1993, sec. 2, pp. 1, 22–23).

The interesting thing about the myth of a white America is that it was the immigrants who helped perpetuate that myth, from the first-generation immigrants in the nineteenth century, whose pride in being American impelled them to suppress their native language for American English, to the Hollywood Jews, most of whom came from Russia and East Europe and who changed their names to something more marketable, more "American," that would fit more conveniently on a marquee. It's ironic that Leonard Bernstein's mentor should have advised him at an early age to change his name to Leonard Burns, and that this mentor should have been Serge Koussevitzky! Who would have thought that Malden Sekulovich, who was born in Indiana, would become familiar as Karl Malden? And who would have thought that Issachar Danielovitch, born in New York State, would turn out to be Kirk Douglas? But is Karl Malden less Malden Sekulovich, Kirk Douglas less Issachar Danielovitch, because of success in Hollywood? Nowadays, actors are proud to write about their humble immigrant beginnings, whereas, a generation ago, these autobiographies would have been forbidden by the studio bosses for fear that such revelations would damage their stars' "all-American" image. Considering the prevailing prejudices of the time, they were probably right. But those days, happily, are over. *Schwarznegger* didn't sound very American at first, but now it does. *Schwarzkopf* was definitively German when we first encountered Elisabeth, but it is now decidedly American in the person of Norman. We are less inclined now to "normalize" our "foreign-sounding" immigrant names than we were in the past. What sounds "American" should be determined by the authentic names of real Americans. Why should *Issachar Danielovitch* be any less American than *Kirk Douglas?* Should we Anglicize *Schwarzkopf* to *Blackhead?*

Visible immigrants receive the brunt of the slurs and the verbal abuse (and not just verbal, as the case of Vincent Chin shows). Once—it was in the late 1980s—a kid on a skateboard (he couldn't have been more than twelve or thirteen) whizzed by my wife and me as we were coming out of a restaurant in a Midwestern town and shouted these words in our faces: "Go home, Chink!" As many times as this has happened, it isn't something I've ever gotten used to. I reflected with sadness on how ignorant the child was and how ignorant his parents must be. But the notion of his assuming that China was my home because I look Chinese infuriated me. I had lived in the United States almost a generation before this thirteen-year old was born, and he is telling me to go home! Still, with the gallows humor that one has to muster up on these occasions, I saw a glimmer of progress in this seemingly never-ending story of prejudice, for it occurred to me to be impressed that this young bigot had at least known (or guessed) the difference between Chinese and Japanese (something which cannot be said of Vincent Chin's killers). In tumultuous times, one is grateful for small favors. Richard Rodriguez is only partially right when he writes, "America is the country where one stops being German, stops being Chinese" (1989, 4). Chinese are visible immigrants; Germans are not. It is harder for a Chinese to stop being foreign in America than it is for a German.

In addition to visible and invisible immigrants, there are "audible" and "inaudible" immigrants. The Macedonian-American founder of the *Daily Macedonian* was an audible immigrant. His accent marks him as someone who speaks a language that, even after half a century, is not natively fluent to him: he appears to be, therefore, a foreigner or an immigrant. Many visible immigrants, however, speak without an accent. My wife and I, American Chinese both, grew up in the United States and went to school in this country. We are not entirely flattered to be told that we speak without an accent. Of course, what the interlocutor indicates by this well-intentioned gaffe is that we are looked on as not being native to this country and that we are therefore not expected to exercise a native command of American English. What this happenstance means is that we are immigrants who are visible but *inaudible*. We can pass for Americans much more easily over the phone than in face-to-face encounters (provided that we don't reveal our ethnic family names). Two instances involving ethnic identity may serve to illustrate this point.

For more than twenty-five years, my father-in-law, a Chinese-American, ran a successful Chinese restaurant in Westport, Connecticut: it was called the West Lake and had quite a distinguished and discriminating clientele. In her high school years, my wife would often work at the restaurant answering the telephone. One customer called up and attempted to order in "Chinese." When my wife was unable to guess what she was saying, the customer abruptly instructed her "to get someone Chinese on the phone." My wife protested that she was Chinese. It's a mistake that the customer would not have made had she seen my wife face to face.

My brother Thomas works as an editor in a publishing house. One interlocutor who had never met him, and who knew him only via correspondence and by telephone, once asked what kind of a name *Eoyang* was; when he told her that he was Chinese, she thought he was joking. Presumably, her image of the Chinese did not include someone who could speak English like a native and be an editor at a publishing house.

I was guilty of a prejudice involving the opposite case, against an "audible immigrant." When I first heard Andrei Codrescu on National Public Radio, his sardonic humor seemed, to me, ill suited to his noticeably accented English. He struck me as a parvenu who had become quickly and modishly Americanized. My reaction was decidedly negative, and, without actually realizing it, I formed a dislike for this "foreigner" who was affecting the American brand of smart-alecky humor. Then, when I met Codrescu and learned that he had grown up in this country and that the American experience was as much his as it was mine, despite his origins and his accented English, I realized that I had made a presumption that, plausible though it may be, was nevertheless wrong and prejudiced. I realized that implicit in my sense of an American identity was the ability to speak unaccented English. Yet, surely, this is unfair when we have no trouble including among bona fide—even famous—Americans those who speak with an accent (Victor Borge and Henry Kissinger come to mind).

I think that it is time to refine the terms describing immigrant generations. *Issei*, *Nisei*, and *Sansei*, designating first-, second-, and third-generation Japanese-Americans, are paradigmatic of our tendency to oversimplify the differences between generations. *First-generation*, for example, is a term that confounds rather than clarifies the situation. A person born elsewhere who comes to this country as a child is technically first-generation, but these first generation immigrants are more likely to be very "Americanized," and they quite naturally think of themselves as "Americans." First-generation immigrants who come to this country as adults, on the other hand, usually have a totally different perspective and are more likely to define themselves in terms of their native identity. It may be useful to distinguish, say, between *American Japanese* or *American Chinese* (no hyphen) and *Japanese-Americans* and *Chinese-Americans*, where the first set of terms refer to those who are Americans of Japanese or Chinese descent but who grew up in the United States, the second set to those whose identities as adults were already established in another culture and who acquired "American" culture after their formative years (cf. Sollors 1986, 208–36).

Within the same generation, there are ethnic Americans and there are American ethnics. Take, for example, the case of Dympna Ugwu-Oju (1993, 40–41). "My friend and I and both our husbands," she writes, "like a majority of our friends, are Nigerians. While we've lived in the United States for most of our adulthood and for all intents and purposes live like Americans, we identify closely with our traditional Ibo culture." She describes the traditional social status of the Ibo woman: "An Ibo woman is born (educated if she is lucky), marries, procreates (a definite must, male children preferably) and dies when her time comes, God rest her soul." Even in America, she tells us, "an Ibo woman has very little personal identity. . . . Our culture [by which she means Ibo culture] takes very little pride in a woman's accomplishment." So, when Ms. Ugwu-Oju's best friend, an Ibo woman, announces that she is leaving her husband after sixteen years of marriage and four children, she is shocked: she can hardly reconcile herself to the news, and there is a rift between the two friends. Ms. Ugwu-Oju's friend looks for sympathy and support for her courageous declaration of independence, but, despite her advocacy of feminist causes in the Third World, Ms. Ugwu-Oju is incredulous at her friend's abandonment of Ibo traditions. With some apprehension, she concludes, "I realized what was going on with my friend. She thinks herself American." The rift is marked, the contrasting perspective could not be more obvious, yet both Ms. Ugwu-Oju and her friend are first-generation immigrants. But it is clear that Ms. Ugwu-Oju is an ethnic American, a Nigerian-American (a Nigerian who immigrated to America), whereas her friend, in allegiance, in sensibility, in cultural identity, is already an American Nigerian (an American of Nigerian descent).

My focus on non-Anglo immigrants is not to deny the importance of the contributions of WASP culture to American history. It is merely to recognize that areas that have been historically neglected need more attention than the "mainstream" elements, which have been more than adequately described. The revisionist tendency to recognize history as "her-story" as well as "his-story" is parallel to the movement to recognize non-Anglo his- and her-stories. Some may remonstrate that to deny the dominating role of WASP culture in American history is to distort history. This is certainly true, although the word *domination* might just as easily be viewed as "oppression." But, if this is true, would the same remonstrator have any qualms about domination coming from other quarters—say, from Latino/Latina culture or African-American? It's interesting how stalwart the defenders of history are except when the tide of history turns against them. The fact that one culture dominates is no reason to argue that it *should have* dominated, or that it *would continue* to dominate, or that it *will continue* to dominate. The resort to involuntary cultural domination is imperialistic. The only ideology that reverts back to a mythical notion of a pure culture, to a single, unadulterated race, is the ideology of National Socialism in Nazi Germany. That pernicious mind-set cannot be repudiated often enough. How pure can Anglo-Saxon culture be, given the hyphen in the name? Even English culture is multicultural. And Adolf Hitler, it is said, suspected that even he had Jewish ancestors.

There's an exchange in the endearing 1979 movie *Breaking Away* that epitomizes the often unsuspected multiculturalism in mainstream "white" American culture. David Stoler has gone on an Italian binge, playing Italian opera, speaking in Italian, following the Cinzano bicycle team. At the dinner table, his father asks, "what's for supper." When David's mother says, "Zucchini," the father launches a tirade against what he calls "-ini" foods—

linguine, fettucine, etc. Exasperated, he commands his wife to serve him some American food: "Give me some French fries!"

There are so many elements in American culture that we take as typically American—from pizza to hamburger to chow mein—but that derive from other cultures. There is an irony in the un-self-reflective absorption of foreign elements in American culture that is belied in the mainstream American suspicion of the foreign. *Breaking Away* reveals something both touching and uplifting about the American experience: its fierce cultural pride and its sense of inferiority toward older, more established cultures. But American culture, represented by the stonecutters in the film, has its own adamantine character, its own often unheralded strengths. Few films in recent years have been more insightfully affirmative about being American than *Breaking Away*. Compared to the vapid chauvinisms of the Rambo films and the atavistic sentimentalities of *Born on the Fourth of July*, *Breaking Away* is as deeply pro-American a film as has been made in decades. It is not coincidental that the script writer, Steve Tesich, was an immigrant from Yugoslavia and that the director, Peter Yates, is English.

Nor should it be forgotten that Michael Curtiz, the director of *Casablanca*, a film that I have characterized as prototypically American, was born in Hungary and christened Mihaly Kertesz. He fled Hungary and worked in France, England, and Scandinavia before coming to the United States, where he was to direct over one hundred films for Warner Brothers in a career that spanned twenty-five years—another immigrant who defines what it means to be an American.[1]

---

1. I am indebted to my friend and colleague Harry Geduld for pointing this detail out to me.

CHAPTER NINE

The Logic and Rhetoric of Racism: False Dyads and True

> If you can meet with Triumph and Disaster
> And treat those two impostors just the same.
> RUDYARD KIPLING, "If"

I once heard an aspiring poet recite an original composition that was nothing but an endless series of paired concepts, like sun and moon, body and soul, heart and mind, light and dark, systole and diastole, heaven and earth, sea and sky, land and water, up and down, left and right, East and West, back and forth, right and wrong, old and new, big and small, black and white, male and female, *yin* and *yang*, in and out, etc., etc. You get the picture. The implicit sense of the poem was that the contrastive pair was a universal structure in everything we see, in everything we experience, in every phenomenon we witness. There is no doubt that these and countless other paired concepts are very familiar, and it would be tempting to see in these pairs a principle of universal nature. But, attractive and suggestive as this endless hunt for dyads may be, the imputation of universality to all dyads would be wrong, for these pairs are not equivalent. Some of them are two things separate from (and seemingly unrelated to) each other, like sun and moon; others are separate and distinct but very much dependent on each other, like body and soul, male and female, *yin* and *yang*; and still others, like up and down, left and right, East and West, are relational notions with no reality of their own, except in their relation with a particular reference point. These dyads made for bad physics, bad philosophy—not to say bad poetry.

Yet more people apply these dyadic concepts in their thinking than any other (although religious thinkers, particularly Christian, are partial to triadic configurations of knowledge). If these dyads are not reflections of some universal principle, why are they so familiar and so pervasive? The answer might be that dyadic thinking may be the most basic tool of intellectual analysis. We need to divide things up in analysis in order to make sense of them. We take things apart to understand the function of each separate part. *To analyze* means "to separate (a material or abstract entity) into constituent parts or elements." But the effectiveness of this tool is no reason to assume that binariness is an inevitable characteristic of all creation (a mistake that some structuralists tended to make). Binariness may not be an attribute of the object we're examining so much as of the approach we find most congenial in understanding that object.

These dyadic contrasts can be further subdivided in value-laden or value free pairs. Up-down, East-West, front-back, ahead-behind may be dyads that are relatively value free, whereas good-evil, right-wrong, and, as we have seen, left-right are by no means value free. Actually, we discover that even neutral pairs have their biases: psycholinguistically, it is better to be up than down, right than left, be ahead than behind (at least in the modern West), in front than in back, etc. However neutral we may think we are with regard to binary pairs (positive/negative poles in electricity), there are inherent biases in our perception of things in dyadic pairs. The point is that the bias is more basic than whether one is biased in favor of one or the other side. What I'm pointing to is a bias that assumes that there are only two sides of an issue to begin with.

Many of our idioms embody this dyadic bias in its conception of issues. "Shakespeare's nothing if not a great writer," is a statement with which most people would tend to agree, but it is a rhetorical statement with a pseudo-logical cast to it. It assumes that there are only two valid alternatives: either that Shakespeare is a great writer or that Shakespeare is nothing. The reduction of the question to these alternatives has no basis. The difference can be seen easily if we take another formulation and say that our alternatives are either that Shakespeare is an English writer or that Shakespeare is not an English writer. This formulation presumes a more plausible and workable duality, there being no third alternative, since the proposition that Shakespeare is an English writer and the proposition that Shakespeare is not an English writer cannot *both* be true. Substitute any writer who is not universally acknowledged as a great writer, and one sees the absurdity of the dyadic presumption. The dyadic formulation of the question itself assumes certain premises: if these premises can be proved true, or if they are self-evident, then the dyadic formulation may be said to be logical; if the premises cannot be true, or if they are false, or if they cannot be proved either true or false, then the dyadic formulation may be said to be rhetorical, without logical warrant.

Consider the outcries during the Vietnam era to dissidents and draft dodgers to "love it or leave it." This dyad fails to consider the possibility of dissidents who leave their country because they love it too much to see it oppressed by tyrants ("love it *and* leave it"), just as it fails to consider those who stay in this country but feel no allegiance toward it ("don't love it and don't leave it"). "If you're not part of the solution, then you're part of the problem" is a tempting formulation that obviously privileges those involved in the solution. But some "solutions," after all, exacerbate the problem, just as some cures are worse than the disease.

There is an interesting distinction to be made among dyadic

contrasts such as these. Some dyads posit two separate identities, like male and female, mind and body. But some dyads are disguised monads: they are not two things but one thing and its absence. Light and dark are not two things, but one: light and the absence of light. Night and day is a cognate contrast.

When we get to dyads like good and evil, however, the situation becomes complex. It is crucial whether we regard them as true dyads or as pseudodyads. Are they really two things or merely one thing, postulated as presence and absence? For example, is evil the mere absence of good, the ignorance of good? Some ancient Greek and Chinese philosophers thought so: they believed that the spread of goodness and virtue and knowledge was what erased evil. Evil was merely straying from the good. Nineteenth-century missionaries felt the same way: by propagating Christianity and civilization, they hoped to eradicate barbarism and brutishness. They saw "primitive" cultures as "benighted": all that had to be done was to shine the light of civilization, and the "uncivilized" would be saved from eternal darkness. Evil was thought of simply as, at bottom, not knowing better.

On the other hand, if we regard good and evil as inherently two things (a plausible heresy for which the Manichaeans were excommunicated seventeen centuries ago), then we subscribe wittingly or unwittingly to the "all good/pure evil" view of the world: we are not then troubled by the complexities of human nature, where no one is entirely virtuous or entirely evil. It is ironic that Christians who have been taught the doctrine of redemption, who have been told the story of the prodigal son, and who have admitted the truth of original sin should nevertheless believe in such simplistic notions as good guys versus bad guys, should subscribe to such notions propagated in perniciously entertaining movie westerns as "the only good Indian is a dead Indian," should support the antinomian pitting of the virtuous faithful against the faithless heathens. The Manichaean view of the world still persists in we-they thinking.

This rash of oversimplistic thinking has been exploited by political rhetoric; it has been nurtured by the media and its insatiable appetite for easily consumed "truths" that preclude true understanding. It has been exacerbated by the short attention span of a generation brought up on television. The authors of commercials, of advertising slogans, and of political diatribes appeal to our dumbest, laziest instincts. They assume that we cannot or will not understand any complexity, so everything is boiled down ideally to a predigested, easy-to-swallow either/or meaning. Examples of this strategy abound: "if you're not with me, then you're against me," "love it or leave it," American or un-American, feminist/antifeminist, conservative/liberal.

True dyads, like the Taoist symbol, deny the validity of this view of the world. Male is not the absence of female; it is another, different, but equally valid presence. (If there is penis envy, then there is also such a thing as womb envy or, as a recent book puts it, "Venus envy)." Our language often invents biased metonymies that represent only one side of the coin. For example, shouldn't there be a female counterpart to the word *patrimony*—because surely we learn as much, if not more, from our mothers as from our fathers about the culture into which we're born? There is, of course, the word *matrimony*, but that has already been taken by another meaning. And, come to think of it, shouldn't there be a male counterpart to *matrimony* as well—because surely the male component in a marriage is as important as the female? These are what I call phantom monoliths; that is, they indicate dualities by indicating only one side.

If there are false dualities that are, in effect, one thing disguised as two, there are also false dualities that are three or more things disguised as two. Somehow it seems rhetorically more definitive to boil everything down to two items; the trouble is that what is rhetorically effective does not always constitute an accurate depiction of reality. The media, however, are more interested in attracting attention than in giving a faithful rendering of complex realities. In the guise of clarity, they contrive oversimplifications. Take as one example the coverage in 8 July 1991 issue of *Time* magazine on multiculturalism. The issues are put in neatly either/or false dualities. The rhetoric is time saving, direct. What is sacrificed, however, is both logic and accuracy: "Put bluntly: Do Americans still have faith in the vision of their country as a cradle of individual rights and liberties, or must they relinquish the teaching of some of these freedoms to further the goals of the ethnic and social groups to which they belong?"

A totally false dichotomy has been erected here. Why should teaching American culture as ensuring individual rights necessarily preclude an emphasis on ethnic and social groups? The critique by ethnic and social groups is that the rhetoric of democracy has been belied by the reality of American history, most conspicuously evinced in the denial of civil rights to American blacks for nearly a century and to American women for a century and a half. The complaint by ethnic groups is not against America but against the disparity between what America has claimed itself to be and what it has actually been. The vision of America as a cradle of individual rights and liberties has been contravened by the facts of history; that vision is reinforced rather than contradicted by emphasis on the immigrant experience and on the goals of ethnic and social groups.

The "either/or" frame of the *Time* account is totally factitious; it's unresponsive to both the logic and the reality of the situation. The article erroneously assumes that, to protect the ideal of America as a truly democratic society, we must pretend that the high principles that the founding fathers espoused have never been violated in our history. However, the truth is that recognizing the violations of those principles is not to undermine them but to affirm them more resolutely and earnestly than they have been affirmed before. Ethnic groups are taking the principles of Western democracy and civil rights seriously; they want the rhetoric of egalitarian rule and equal opportunity to be replaced with a reality that ensures what the high-sounding principles promise.

The two thrusts—toward the ideals of democracy and those of ethnic inclusiveness—are not at odds with one another, except in the slipshod thinking of hurried reporters meeting a deadline or of demagogues more interested in rhetoric than in realities. They are not either/or propositions; they are both/and propositions. To achieve the ideal of democratic principles is to realize the identities of the ethnic and social groups that compromise a democracy.

The cover headline of the *Time* issue is yet another instance of a factitious dualism: "American kids are getting a new—and divisive—view of Thomas Jefferson, Thanksgiving and the Fourth of July." Why must an awareness of multiculturalism be inherently divisive? Does the physicist—say, a Newton—think it "divisive" to refract ordinary light into the colors of the rainbow? And what kind of nondivisiveness is claimed for an America that does not recognize the diversity in its history? The logic would seem to be to accept the traditional view of American history or to be considered divisive or, worse, disloyal. The logic does not differ greatly from that behind Joseph McCarthy's witch-hunts and his insistence on loyalty oaths. Accept the old view, or else you will be considered divisive. Sign the loyalty oath, or you will be considered a Communist. This view of national security involves a justification for lying whenever doing so is in the interest of "national security," an argument that alas, not only captivates a good portion of our population but characterizes the thinking of several self-styled "patriots" as well. The sad thing is that they forget that this country is the only one in the world where one can be critical and still express, *by that criticism*, one's allegiance to the ideals of the country. Art Buchwald has acknowledged that he could thrive only in America, for not only does he, like other political satirists, criticize this country incessantly, he even makes fun of it. In any other country, especially in totalitarian countries, he would be vilified and persecuted as disloyal, but here in America, on the contrary, he reaps lavish rewards and is, in fact, lionized. No one, however, questions Art Buchwald's love for, or his loyalty to, the United States of America.

The trouble with the logic of dyadic rhetoric is that it posits a false alternative: a kind of "heads I win tails you lose" proposition. There is only the mirage of a choice. There are many versions of this one-pretending-to-be-two imperative: "Believe—or be damned!" "Winning isn't everything, it's the only thing!" "If you're not part of the solution, then you're part of the problem." Each of these propositions is emotionally charged: these are impassioned declarations extorting—rather than exhorting—assent. Two alternatives are offered, one of which is either nonexistent or unacceptable. They are demands for positive action: "Believe!" "Win!" "Solve the problem!" There's nothing wrong with these expressions as honest rhetorical exhortations, but they are misleading and dishonest when presented as basic logic because they offer a phantom choice. That's also the trouble with black-and-white rhetoric.

When I mentioned to a colleague that I was writing something on multiculturalism, his immediate response was, "I hope you're against it!" That is reflective of an unthinking approach to the issue: take a side, and then you don't have to be troubled to think about the complexities of the issue. My answer, both true and evasive, was, "I am both for and against it." I am for the recognition of the historical fact of multiculturalism even if that fact has been neglected by traditional histories, but I am against the monolithic insistence on "politically correct" versions of multiculturalism. There are some who will think my position contradictory and the two positions I espouse mutually exclusive: to them, I respond by saying that, indeed, I believe, and I'll be damned as well; that winning can be learned only by losing and that, sometimes, winning *is* losing (ever hear of Pyrrhic victories?). Some observers are convinced that there was a causal connection between George Bush's victory in the Persian Gulf War of 1991, followed inevitably by a sense of complacency, and his unexpected defeat in the 1992 presidential elections. The Persion Gulf War was certainly a triumph for George Bush, but it might also have planted the seeds of his defeat.

In other words, I refuse to accept the proposition that there are only two alternatives (or, what is worse, only one alternative) to any issue. (The expression *only one alternative* may seem to be a contradiction in terms—after all, *alternative* already infers the existence of at least two possibilities, but it exactly describes the extortionary pseudodualities that we've been examining.) This penchant in Western civilization for a yes/no view of reality has many antecedents, from the trial by combat in the medieval period to the duel in the arenas, including the courtrooms and playing fields, of later eras. We like decisiveness, whether or not that accords with reality. The abhorrence of ties in American sports—the proverbial justification, interesting for its implicit chauvinism, is that "it's like kissing your sister"—is a reflection of this requirement that there be a definitive outcome within a finite period of time. This has led to the efforts to reduce ties in such sports as basketball, baseball, football, hockey, soccer, tennis: there are tiebreakers, sudden deaths, overtimes, extra innings, free kicks, all to avoid the possibility of an indecisive outcome. But isn't life full of indecisive outcomes, so-called Mexican standoffs? And history provides us with more examples of irresolutions than clear-cut victories and defeats. That clear-cut victories and defeats are more memorable and easier to write about sometimes misleads us into thinking that they are a pervasive feature of mundane reality.

Combative dualities are an inextricable part of the American mind-set, and, as a result, we are accustomed to thinking that the very structure of understanding is dual, that duality is in the very nature of things. This is very far from the truth, as anyone believing in trinitarian godheads can attest. There are, of course, other numerical paradigms: four seasons, twelve months, twenty-four hours, sixty minutes, ten fingers. But the paradigm of twoness in American culture predominates.

In America, coalitions—the joining together of disparate groups with common interests—have been the prime factor in our success, whether in the tradition of political compromise, or in the mobilization of different constituencies behind a single candidate or a particular piece of legislation, or in the coming together of the original thirteen very different sovereign states in order to form "a more perfect union." The greatest achievements occurred when conflicting interests were put aside for a higher cause, as in the national effort during the Second World War, which brought all segments of American society together against common enemies—Republicans and Democrats, management and labor, men and women. (World wars are, of course, examples on an international scale of the meretriciousness of combative dualities.) The greatest disasters in American history, on the other hand, where good people died on both sides, was the Civil War, which developed out of a destructive, combative duality of mind in both the North and the South, and the Vietnam War, which prompted a polarized mentality that needlessly and erroneously pitted patriotism and morality on opposite sides. Perhaps with the resolutions effected between F. W. De Klerk and Nelson Mandela in South Africa, between Yasir Arafat and Itzhak Rabin in the West Bank and the Golan Heights, and the beginnings of negotiations, whether secret or public, between Sinn

Fein in Northern Ireland and the British government, people are beginning to realize the futility of combative dualities as well as to recognize their inherent falsity.

There is a pseudoduality, a false dyad, forming today with regard to political correctness. One complex position is being—whether advertently, by the mischievous, or inadvertently, by the unwary—bifurcated into two, with biases determining which position is to be chosen. Unnecessary conflicts are thus generated, which are fodder to the media and to the ideologues who want no reconciliation with "separated brethren." Disagreements are manufactured where, at bottom, there is no disagreement. And there are ironies: some of those who wish a more comprehensive and truthful version of American history, one that includes the contributions of its minority cultures, are assuming the same fascism of the mind against which they are declaiming. The ties that bind are being replaced by the lies that separate. It isn't a matter of what is "correct" or "incorrect"—for that posits without foundation a yes/no answer to the complex questions of reality. To ask for a revisionist view of American history is not to repudiate the ideals of the founding fathers but to affirm them with a greater commitment.

Those in favor of a version of history that reflects the contribution of ethnic groups need not discard the contributions of the English immigrants—the Washingtons, the Franklins, and the Jeffersons—to the founding of this country. It is not an either/or proposition to insist on a greater recognition of the pluralistic character of early American history: there ought to be more recognition of the German, French, and Spanish influences in the formation of precolonial and colonial America. The help of the French during the Revolutionary War is well known, but Spain's help was also crucial. In the nineteenth century, the settlement of the Scandinavians in the north Midwest states, the French in northern New England and the Mississippi Delta, the

Africans (albeit against their will) in the South, the Germans through the Midwest, the Spanish in Florida and the Southwest; in the late nineteenth and early twentieth centuries, the Asians in California, the East European Jews in southern California—recognizing these historical facts is not a distortion of history. The multicultural movement is dedicated to recuperating the multiplicity of American history, which includes German pumpernickel, French toast, and Jewish rye as well as Wonder white bread. One man's ravioli is another man's potsticker.

There are lessons to be learned from nature. An available parable comes from the realm of science, in particular from agronomy and agricultural engineering. With so much of the ecosystem being destroyed, wild strains of agricultural plants are disappearing at an alarming rate. In the era of the "Green Revolution," when many high-yield crop strains have been developed, one would think that wild, uncultivated strains of agricultural plants would be unnecessary. On the contrary, it turns out that it is vital to save wild strains of agricultural plants, not for any sentimental environmental concerns, but for the very protection of the strains that have produced the Green Revolution. But why is their preservation so necessary when they are not the hybrid, high-yield, pest-resistant strains that are used all over the world? The answer is that genetically uniform crop strains are "much more vulnerable to catastrophic destruction by insects, fungi, bacteria and viruses" (*New York Times*, 25 June 1991). In the past, however, infestations of pests, insects, bacteria, and viruses, would have been only a local problem since the agricultural stock varied from region to region. Now, with worldwide use of the same hybrid varieties, what would have been only a local disaster would very quickly become a global catastrophe. Only selective cross-breeding with wild varieties of plants will reduce the vulnerability of the high-yield strains to new attacks. Some of the wild strains have highly desirable characteristics, such as a natural resistance to pests (which obviates the need for chemical pesticides, which damage not only the environment but sometimes the crops themselves).

The argument for diversity comes down to this: to preserve a way of life, no matter who might enjoy it, or to preserve one's own way of life, no matter who might be denied access to it, is to doom it to extinction. Truly, to preserve a way of life is to adapt it to new circumstances, to modify it, and to make it new again. This is the way every tradition survives, by organic re-generations, not by archival arrests.

The roots of prejudice are imbedded deep in human nature, and the paradox of America is that, while, on the one hand, it is dedicated to individual rights, nevertheless it seeks from each individual the collective allegiance to an idea that protects the rights of *all* individuals. The abstract devotion to individual rights sometimes becomes difficult when those rights are exercised by unsavory or despicable individuals. The basic conviction of the founding fathers was the supremely inspired idea of making something abstract memorably specific and concrete: that one's own rights depended on how well the rights of others were protected. The legal system, the Constitution, the political system, at least in theory, are predicated on "Three Musketeers" ("all for one, and one for all") philosophy. This philosophy is easy to carry out when the Three Musketeers are congenial, charming, and likable people. But it becomes difficult for many people when the other "musketeers" are unfamiliar, unfriendly, hostile, and disagreeable. The philosophy does not, however, sanction subjective qualifiers, what might be called *goodness* modifiers: it does not specify "all for one (provided that he or she is a good person or a likable person)"; it says simply "all for one" with the implication of "anyone," regardless of race, color, creed, or temperament. Contrary to the implied interpretation in some quarters, the Constitution does not say, "We, the *good* people of the United States of America." The vindication of the demo-cratic principle in politics and of the egalitarian principle in law is precisely demonstrated when the person whose rights are protected is *dis*liked by the community. It takes no profound principle to protect the individual rights of the popular and the admired and the virtuous: democratic, egalitarian principles are not needed for that. Instinctive human nature will gravitate naturally to the defense of the good, the attractive, and the virtuous.

I find disturbing the difficulty that some Americans have appre-ciating Henry David Thoreau. Undoubtedly, he was a thor-oughly unpleasant, self-centered person, decidedly not "a team player," and certainly not friendly. A nation of Henry David Thoreaus could not survive very long. Yet it is precisely relevant that Thoreau was off-putting, that he was—either by nature or by design—belligerent and pugnacious. There is a confusion between the idea of egalitarian government and the notion of popularity. The strength of a democracy lies not only in the collective wisdom of its citizens but also in the resoluteness of its mavericks. The majority of one is what keeps the majority of the many honest. A strong democracy will depend as much on vocal minorities of one as on active majorities of many. If we cannot protect the rights of the least of us, then the greatest among us have no rights.

CHAPTER TEN

Coat of Many Colors:
The Myth of a White America

But the things you will learn from the Yellow an' Brown
They'll 'elp you a lot with the White!

RUDYARD KIPLING, *The Ladies*

I n the traditional translations of the story of Joseph in the Book of Genesis, the coat of many colors figures prominently.[1] This gift, which Jacob confers on Joseph, his favorite son, is emblematic of Joseph's privileged state; it is the symbol against which the envy of his brothers is directed. To make matters worse, Joseph tells his brothers about a dream—and, given Joseph's particular gift for interpreting dreams, this cannot be a frivolous dream—in which his sheaf of grain rose up and stood upright while theirs formed a ring around his and bowed down to it (Gen. 37:7). His brothers are resentful: "And they hated him all the more for his talk about his dreams" (Gen. 37:8). A second dream makes the symbolism of hegemony and power even more explicit: the sun and eleven stars bowed down to him (Gen. 37:9). Now, Jacob is incensed: "'What is the meaning,' he asked him, ' of this dream of yours? Shall I and your mother and your brothers come bowing to you to the ground?'" Later in the

---

1. Another traditional version is the "coat with sleeves"; neither version is deemed very accurate by modern biblical scholarship, which translates the original Hebrew as "ornamented tunic" (see Speiser, 1964, 289). (All quotations from Genesis are from Speiser's text.)

story, the coat of many colors also figures prominently as "evidence": the brothers daub it with blood and present it as "proof" that Joseph has been devoured by wild beasts.

This biblical tale may be a parable of arrogance on the part of Joseph and jealousy on the part of his brothers. But the Bible makes it clear that Joseph is Yahweh's (God's) favorite as well, for, when he is sent to Egypt, he prospers, and, when he is thrown into jail because Potiphar's wife falsely accuses him of rape, Yahweh blesses him: "And whatever he undertook, Yahweh made prosper" (Gen. 39:23).

The latter part of the story depicts Joseph's spectacular rise to power in Egypt, his prophetic gifts being translated into economic power, wielded with an authority second only to Pharaoh's. Eventually, Joseph is able, even during the seven years of famine that he had predicted, to bring to Egypt Jacob and all his surviving offspring—including the brothers who, at the outset of the story, had victimized Joseph and to whom, ironically, Joseph owes his subsequent good fortune.

The story of Joseph and his brothers is well worth pondering in the context of race relations in the United States. "Whites" in America are, in a positive sense, reminiscent of Joseph: they have been favored by history; they enjoy the highest standard of living; they have "foretold" the future more accurately than their brethren; and they have the gift of oneiric creativity, of making their dreams come true. Their shrewdness in economic affairs reminds one of Joseph's spectacular land acquisitions in Egypt, augmenting Pharaoh's holdings by exploiting those who had been reduced to poverty and starvation by the famine, offering part of the ample provisions stored up during the seven years of plenty to buy land.

The coat of many colors turns out to be a doubly ambivalent gift: a token of Jacob's love, it brings down on Joseph the envy and hostility of his brothers, which in turn motivates their dire

153

plot against him; but it also leads to his exile in Egypt as well as the ultimate deliverance of Jacob's family during the years of famine. The image of "white" has had the same import in the United States. Emblem of privilege and favoritism, symbol of suspected arrogance, the insignia of political domination and ambition, "whites" in America for most of our history are very reminiscent of Joseph in a negative sense as well: opportunistic in their ambitions, ruthless in capitalizing on their economic opportunities, manipulative in the marketplace of ideas and of human resources. Their success has also made whites the target of a great deal of animosity, from the "have-nots" both in the United States and in the world. "White America"—like Joseph—is the envy of the world, for both positive and negative reasons, to both favorable and unfavorable effect.

To meditate on the story of Joseph might be a more fruitful approach to an appreciation of white American culture than wading through the polemics of race relations or sifting through volumes of less than dispassionate rhetoric, for there is much to admire as well as to deplore about white America. But the sad truth is that most analyses polarize themselves unduly by depicting the white American either as the devil incarnate (Ahab's version of Moby Dick) or as an angel of purity personified (Snow White and her seven—ethnic?—dwarfs). There is another connection between Joseph's coat of many colors and the color white: while common custom "sees" white as a color among other colors, the science of optics tells us that white is a figment of our visual imaginations. There is no color white, per se; what we see as the color white is a composite of many colors. White can be thought of as a coat of many colors.

It is the composite nature of white, and the ambivalent character of Joseph in the biblical tale, that we must understand if any light is to be shed on the conundrum of race relations in America. Much of what is regarded as mainstream "white" culture in the United States comes from ethnic origins that are decidedly un-English and un-European. A proper definition of *white culture* in America must take into account the nonwhite elements as well.

Those who are wary of the recognition of America's multicultural past, who insist on seeing such discriminations as discriminatory, often appeal to the importance of a common belief system to the very survival of America as a nation. The concepts of unity in diversity and *e pluribus unum* (one out of many) are often compromised when the country as a whole is under attack. Opposition parties historically rally around the president during times of military crisis, and differences of opinion are not as easily tolerated when the polity as a whole is threatened. The debate in Congress over whether the United States should enter the Persian Gulf War was an inspiring moment in American democracy, for, whatever side of the issue one stood on, few challenged the loyalty of those who disagreed with what turned out to be the majority view (which constituted a healthy change from the prevailing wind during the Vietnam War). Justifications of unconstitutional actions in terms of "national security" did not die out with the perfidies of Richard Nixon: others have invoked the concept since. It is a disturbing kind of patriotism that believes it necessary to lie to the American people in order to protect their freedoms.

Is it un-American to recognize one's roots? Is it un-American to identify the foreign sources of one's talent and vision? Has there ever been an America that wasn't anything but the sum total of immigrant dreams? Why is it necessary to "white out" one's immigrant origins in order to become American? Imperceptibly, a myth has grown up in this country that a native-born American is more American than someone who is not native born. Some of us have forgotten that one of the complaints lodged against King George III in the Declaration of Independence was that he obstructed "laws for naturalization of foreigners."

Naturalization strikes me as a uniquely American concept. Counterparts in other countries include *sinicization* for Chinese, *anglicization* for English culture *gallicization* for French. But there is something distinct about *naturalization* in America: the word means: "to invest (an alien) with the rights and privileges of a citizen." Whereas the other terms identify the process by which the foreigner acquires the native culture in each respective country, the word *naturalization* merely points to the process by which the rights and privileges of a citizen are conferred on a foreigner. Nowhere is it said, neither in the Declaration of Independence nor in the Constitution, that one has to give up one's native (foreign) culture in order to become or be American. The act of naturalization is not cultural but institutional: the recognition of, and allegiance to, the basic principles of American government is all that is required of an American citizen or of an alien who wants to be "naturalized." In other words, anyone who is willing to subscribe to the ideals of the American form of society, whatever her ethnic origins or social status, can become an American. The most natural American is also a "naturalized" American: the problem is that some native-born Americans are not as familiar with the institutional history of America as some immigrants, who have to learn the Declaration of Independence and the Constitution practically by heart in order to qualify for "naturalization." Being born American is not the only way to become American: as a nation that prides itself on our colonial history and that believes in the importance that Jefferson attached to the laws of "naturalization of foreigners," we can ill afford to forget that.

I have lived in a small Midwestern community for more than twenty-five years. Once I had some business to conduct with a local merchant. Our discussions reached an amicable conclusion.

Unbeknownst to me, a colleague happened to visit the same merchant shortly after my visit to inquire about the same project. The merchant repeated what he had told me, and then, scarcely able to contain his curiosity, he asked my colleague about me: "Your friend, he's . . . he's not from around here, is he?" In hearing my friend's report, I was touched that the local merchant was too shy to admit that I looked a little different from his usual customers. Perhaps he was curious about *which* country I came from. In retrospect, I appreciated his discretion about asking me: obviously, he was made somewhat uncertain because my English sounded thoroughly native.

Which raises the interesting question, What does *from around here* mean? I later found out that this merchant had moved into the community fifteen years after I had arrived. Yet, I could not deny that, notwithstanding our actual tenure in town, I would always be perceived as being "not from around here" whereas he could always appear to belong, no matter how recent a new-comer he was. The contrast is that he would look at home virtually anywhere in the United States, no matter how recently he took up residence, whereas I would always look as if I were "not from around here," no matter how long I had lived in one place.

There is a Custer's Last Stand mentality among certain de-fenders of WASP culture: they are beleaguered by foreign com-petition in the marketplace, beset by waves of immigrants from all countries, and besieged by assaults on their values and pre-cepts by radical activists. The pressures against the white major-ity in the United States have escalated to such an extent that even moderate white Americans are feeling threatened by the onslaught of ethnic and racial rhetoric. They are circling the wagons against the intellectual and political tyrannies of "politi-cal correctness." Typically, profoundly complex issues are being co-opted by oversimplifications to produce a great deal of fric-tion and heat, yielding very little understanding or light. We are being asked to choose up sides, as in a pickup stickball game, but the false dichotomies are mischievous, if not malicious. Unless we sort out the issues and see them clearly, the disputes will fester and conflicts multiply without any real progress toward solutions. The sad thing is that it is all so unnecessary.

If the hypocricies and deceits of WASP culture have been amply documented, perhaps it is time to focus on the unique WASP contribution to human civilization. Whatever other cultures, each with its own virtues, have to claim, in no other than white Anglo-Saxon Protestant culture has the tradition of democracy and freedom been so passionately articulated. From the Magna Carta to Jimmy Carter (a peanut farmer who became president), the commitment to egalitarian forms of government is that culture's most glorious contribution to civilization. The great civilizations and cultures of the world each have their particular achievements, but in none has the idea of egalitarian rule been pursued with as much dedication, imagination, and sacrifice as in white Anglo-Saxon Protestant culture. These principles are the higher cause that must unite the various cultural and political constituencies in these United States.

These are the principles that have allowed the various mixes of people to unite in a common cause, however disparate their customs and backgrounds, however at odds their belief systems and religions, however contradictory and contrary their political views. But, if this is the achievement of WASP culture, then, ironically, it cannot be undermined by an interpretation of equal opportunity that is restricted only to WASP culture. These principles become a travesty when "we, the people" must be interpreted as "we, the white people," or "we, the rich people," or "we, the male people." And, so long as the reality in America fails to redeem the promises made in the Declaration of Independence and the Constitution, the very achievement of WASP culture is undermined. There is a quantum leap in this magnanimity of vision, greater than that of the Greeks, whose definition of freedom was not extended to their slaves; greater than that of the Romans, whose notion of power did not include women; greater than that of the Chinese, whose notion of culture did not recognize the contribution of the foreigner—for the crowning achievement of the WASP vision of the world is that it confers on all peoples, not just WASPs, "the right to life, liberty, and the pursuit of happiness." The multicultural vision, therefore, does nothing to diminish the achievement of WASP culture or the triumph of Western civilization; on the contrary, it demonstrates irrefutably the genius of this uniquely compelling vision of humanity.

It is as wrong to presume that all nonwhites are actually or incipiently "antiwhite" as it is foolish, categorically wrong, to dismiss all whites as racists and cultural bigots. Those who have attributed the term *political correctness* to those in favor of the multicultural movement wish to discredit that movement, and those in the movement who believe in political correctness do not truly understand multiculturalism. The issue is not to replace a white orthodoxy with a nonwhite orthodoxy. The issue of multiculturalism should be about culture rather than politics; it should be concerned with sensitivities rather than categorical correctness. Being politically correct is no guarantee that ethnic sensitivities will not be offended: as a minority, I am more impressed by the human concern of someone who might be politically incorrect than by the doctrinaire liberal formulas of the politically correct. Minorities are not interested in correct behavior; what they want is responsive behavior. The notion of *political correctness* is at bottom intensely insulting to minorities because it suggests that ethnic individuals be treated "by the book" and that there is a right and a wrong way to deal with other human beings. Nothing could be more obnoxious than a handbook of political correctness; it reflects the same thinking as a manual on the care and feeding of animals. As a minority, I may wish to be treated kindly, or candidly, or circumspectly, or courteously, or sympathetically, or considerately, or honestly; but God spare me from anyone bent on treating me "correctly."

If *multiculturalism* means anything, it also includes WASP culture as a primary component of the American experience. To insist that the whole story of American history be told is not the same thing as erasing the contribution of white Americans to that history. Indeed, just as one argues that the black contributions to white culture deserve to be recognized, the genetic contributions of whites to black culture must also be acknowledged. If there is nothing pure about white culture, there is also nothing pure about black culture. Although no official statistics are available, a considerable number of blacks in the United States have at least one white among their ancestors. The fact that many blacks were the offspring of rape and miscegenation was perhaps the reason to be discreet about the "white" genes interspersed among the "black." There is ample inferential proof of the infusion of white blood in the black population, often from the very people who wish to downgrade blacks as inferior.[2]

In Louisiana, state law defines anyone with one part black blood out of sixty-four as being black. If we assume as many as sixty-four great-great-great-great-grandparents, that means that anyone with as few as *one* black ancestor out of these sixty-four is considered, according to Louisiana law, black. In other words, the sixty-three other great-great-great-great-grandparents could be white, but they wouldn't count. One would still be black in

2. Chapter 10 of Ralph Ellison's *The Invisible Man* opens with a description of a paint factory with the sign, "Keep America Pure with Liberty Paints," and goes on to explain how ten drops of *black* paint added to white paint makes "Optic White," "the purest white that can be found," "as white as George Washington's Sunday-go-to-meetin' wig," the paint that's "heading for a national monument," "that'll cover just about anything!" I am indebted to Agnes Moreland Jackson of Pitzer College for reminding me of this detail.

the eyes of Louisiana law. Leaving aside the ethical and eugenic dimensions of this law, its existence, and the severely prejudicial ratio that it enshrines, would suggest a high incidence of blacks with one or more white progenitors. Such a law would not have been enacted were the number of blacks with white blood negligible. The implicit cut-off imposed by this law is that, if one had a great-great-great-great-great-grandparent who was black (in other words, if a black could prove that 127 out of 128 progenitors of that generation were white), one would be considered, in the eyes of Louisiana law, white. However, if one could do no better than sixty-three out of sixty-four progenitors in the subsequent generation, then one had to be considered legally black. Somehow it seems so pointless a distinction: one is considered black if one of the sixty-four ancestors six generations ago was black, but one isn't considered black if 127 of the 128 ancestors seven generations ago were white!

Nothing betrays the myth of white purity more than these ridiculously persnickety distinctions. One can fairly ask about the validity of a distinction that rests on such flimsy genealogical grounds, especially when most Americans can hardly identify their ancestors past a few generations, much less six or seven.[2]

Multiculturalism must also recognize the proportion of white progenitors in the black population. White is a culture too. It is as foolish to be for or against whites as it is to be for or against blacks. The dynamics of prejudice apply in any direction. The black who stereotypes whites is just as racist as the white who stereotypes blacks. It is racism that all races should be against, and there is no way to eradicate another person's racism by opposing it with your own.

What we should all be against is the "whitewash" mentality. *Whitewash* is my term for leaving out salient parts of the truth and then glossing over those omissions; the appropriation of a valid cause for an invalid purpose. *Whitewash* is the dedicated insistence on ideals with no regard to how those ideals are controverted and undermined in reality. *Whitewash* is the false attribution of treason to those who will not accept the predominant ideology. Whites are not the only ones capable of whitewash. There are the "Oreos" and the "bananas" and the "coconuts"—the blacks who are black on the outside and white on the inside; the Asians who are yellow on the outside and white on the inside; and the Latinos/Latinas or East Indians who are brown on the outside but white on the inside. These intercultural symbols indicate a white heart in a skin of color, and they are instances of what might be called *internal whitewash*—where the psyche has been brainwashed into thinking that one is white when one isn't.

There is also the phenomenon of the *external whitewash*—where one "puts on a white face," as it were. There are ethnics who have mastered the art of "whiteface"—playing the white man's game to get ahead in white society. The interesting thing is that whites scarcely notice these racial caricatures, and they are not as offended by blacks playing in "whiteface" as blacks are by whites playing in blackface.[3] Richard Pryor, for example, gets as many laughs from whites as blacks imitating a "honky." Could it be that blackface unfairly caricatures an oppressed people whereas whiteface merely acknowledges the dominant culture? (There is an entire psychology of humor to be explored that would explain why ethnics insulting themselves can be funny but nonethnics insulting ethnics is not funny—except to bigots.)

But there are more subtle forms of ethnic whitewash, in which individuals take umbrage behind their ethnic masks rather than assume responsibility for their own limitations and failures. We have all met such moral hypocrites: those who cry "racism" at

3. Franz Fanon, in *The Wretched of the Earth*, and Jean Genet, in *The Blacks*, explored the symbolic meanings of acting in whiteface.

the drop of a hat, despite the fact that others of the same race have succeeded in the same job or in the same situation; those who cry anti-Semitism, even when Jews have preceded them in the same profession; and those who cry sexism to avoid admitting their own shortcomings. The irony is that those most often offended by these "cry-wolfers" are those minority individuals who are successful and who achieved their success, sometimes against racism, through extra hard work and dedication. The ambivalence of these minority individuals is profound: they hate the racism that has made their road to success difficult, but they feel indebted to those very difficulties for making them better and tougher than their white counterparts. Shelby Steele touches on some of these perspectives in *The Content of Our Character* (1990).

I am reminded of an incident years ago in New York City, when my wife and I lived in a small one-and-half-room apartment on Riverside Drive. Late one Saturday night, actually, it was early Sunday morning, around three o'clock, I woke up to the thumping and shaking of loud music and dancing next door. Bleary eyed, I got up and knocked on my neighbor's door. An African opened up, amid gales of merriment. When I said that the party was perhaps a bit too boisterous, my African neighbor accused me of racism. I suspected that this response was his knee-jerk response in all such situations, and he was not even disconcerted to notice that, with my Chinese face, I did not at all resemble the white racists he was in the habit of impugning.[4]

It is eyewash to teach the Fourteenth Amendment and not point out its violation throughout American history since it was passed in 1866. One can never be reminded too often of the text of the Fourteenth Amendment: "All persons born or naturalized

4. Which is not to ignore the fact of antiblack racism in China. In 1981, there were riots in Nanjing and in Beijing caused by antiblack feeling.

in the United States, and subject to the jurisdiction thereof, are citizens of the United States and of the State wherein they reside. No State shall make or enforce any law which shall abridge the privileges or immunities of the citizens of the United States; nor shall any State deprive any persons of life, liberty, or property, without due process of law; nor deny to any person within its jurisdiction the equal protection of the law" (section 1). The teaching of history that underscores the magnanimity and the nobility of the Fourteenth Amendment, yet neglects the internment of sixty thousand American citizens of Japanese descent in 1942, is whitewashing reality and making a travesty of history. And to read "No State shall . . . deny to any person within its jurisdiction the equal protection of the law" without any concern for the differential proportions by which blacks are sentenced to the death penalty, especially when whites are the victims, without recognizing the repeated abrogation of the rights of Native Americans in broken treaty after broken treaty, without acknowledging the injustices perpetrated on Latino/ Latina immigrants, especially those characterized cynically by fruit growers as "wetbacks," is whitewashing the truth. We cannot celebrate lofty sentiments and at the same time ignore instances in which those sentiments are conveniently disregarded.

There is also a blitheness among some whites about the ethnic experience, a blindness that indicates that they have no sense of what it is to live day after day in one's own country and yet be made to feel a stranger in it. Only minorities have experienced the special hurt of living in a country and being told by someone much younger that they don't belong here. Whites who know nothing of this experience might be instructed by a German-American friend who traveled in Japan and was stunned to find herself, for the first time in her life, in the minority. Whites who have not been alienated in their own country blithely suggest that ethnics are wrong to point to their own traditions; they insist that it is divisive and separatist to use such hyphenated designations as African-American, Chinese-American, Italian-American, etc. Two examples from popular journalism, from respected and intelligent commentators on the American scene, will suffice to illustrate this blindness.

The first comes from Marilyn Vos Savant: "I believe one of the greatest threats to the stability of the United States may well be the declining number of people who call themselves Americans. I wonder how long the hyphenation of nationalities can continue without bringing the hyphenations of loyalties. Whenever people ask me whether I'm a French-American, for example, because of my name, it irritates me, and I tell them, 'No. I was born in this country, I'm a citizen, and I'm an American!'" (*Parade Magazine*, 26 May 1991). Ms. Vos Savant is totally oblivious to the experience of non-European immigrants or the descendants of non-European immigrants: they aren't even asked the hyphenized version of their nationality. If they look "Oriental," they are asked, "Are you Chinese or Japanese?" (Of course, the more circumspect and thoughtful ask where your ancestors come from.) We are not asked, "Are you Chinese-American or Japanese-American?" Indeed, in the eyes of some, we are seen as not being American.

And then there are times when Americans of Chinese descent are misidentified at the peril of their lives. In 1989, James Liu in Raleigh, North Carolina, a Chinese-American, was taken to be Vietnamese, so two pool-hall bullies bashed his head in, as an act of vengeance for the trauma that they, and America, had suffered as a result of the Vietnam War. In 1981, Vincent Chin was erroneously taken for Japanese, and two autoworkers, disgruntled at being put out of work (by the Japanese, they thought, not by mismanaged American corporations), beat his brains in.

Vincent Chin and Jim Liu would have been proud to be called, simply, American, but their assailants were, evidently, unwilling to recognize their citizenship.

In fact, it may come as a surprise to Marilyn Vos Savant that many ethnic Americans do not like the hyphen because it makes them feel like second-class citizens; the hyphen represents Americans whose citizenship is somehow compromised. Most ethnics would be delighted to eliminate the hyphen as well as the ethnic marker and call themselves simply Americans. What is to Ms Vos Savant a choice—to be called a hyphenated American or to be called, simply, American—is, unfortunately, not an option for those who are physiognomically at variance with what, mythically, an American is "supposed" to look like. Vos Savant has the situation on backward: the divisive forces—racism—impose the need for hyphenated Americans; the labels are not assumed voluntarily. But, since the hyphenation has become inevitable, some of the militant ethnics (much like the blacks of the 1960s) have insisted on the label as a reminder of white racism. Vos Savant wants to remove the symptom without attending to the disease.

A similar form of *whitewash*—here its cognate is *Americanization*—may be found in the writing of Peggy Noonan, speechwriter for Presidents Reagan and Bush. Too savvy politically to offend any constituency, Noonan is, on the whole, positive about the recent influx of immigrants—"the biggest . . . since the great wave that ended in the 1920's." Noonan puts forth a concept of *Americanism* that she characterizes as "the Sunday stew—rich, various and roiling, and all of it held together by a good strong broth" (1991, 39). After celebrating the successes of several recent immigrants, Noonan goes on to say, "Nationwide, the small shops the immigrants run create thousands of jobs and contribute billions to the economy. In return, the newcomers get the possibility of dreams. But these dreams aren't free. There's a price to pay: once you're here, you have to become American-ized." Just what does *becoming Americanized* mean? If it means to become acculturated to WASP culture (as it does in the minds of many, and not only in the minds of whites), then Americani-zation is merely another form of cultural hegemony. Noonan avoids this ethnocentric interpretation: she talks about the "moral and philosophical underpinnings of what they've joined, the things that keep us together. These include the reasons we fought the Revolutionary War and the Civil War, the meaning of the civil-rights movement and the reasons we have sent armies across oceans to liberate other nations. To know what we were is to know who we are."

These are fine sentiments, and few would take issue with them. It's only when one looks at the substance and the concrete examples of what Noonan talks about that this rhetoric begins to sound hollow. She says, "This is why we must not permit school texts to imply, as some do, that 'America was founded by white male Euros who broke from Britain over taxes but retained slaves, and two centuries later the liberation is not complete because racism is still rampant.'" The "we" in "we must not permit" betrays Noonan's provinciality, for this "we" is evidently addressed to orthodox white Americans, not to blacks, whose role in the Revolutionary War has been obscured by the previous textbooks, and not to Japanese-Americans, who fought in the all-Nisei 442d Regimental Combat team in World War II (one of the most decorated in the war), and not to the Japanese-Americans whose lands were confiscated and whose civil rights were violated. And Noonan says nothing to contradict the ver-sion of American history she sneers at. America as the history books present it *was* founded by white male Euros, wasn't it? And where is the egalitarian spirit in Noonan's exclusive and imperious "we"? Some of the "we's" are committed to rewriting American history by telling the truth, and we seek no one's permission to do so. As Noonan says, "To know what we were is to know who we are." But that's exactly what "revisionist" history is after: to truly know what we truly were. How can she be against a more accurate depiction of America's history, and why does she characterize this search for more accurate history as "sour revisionism"? Are we talking about ideologies, party lines, or the facts of history? Why is a revision of knowledge revisionism? The whole notion of revisionism smacks of totalitarian excuses to discipline the wayward. And why should the restoration of truth ever be considered sour? Is it divisive, sour, and spoilsport to insist that the errors of previous scientific textbooks be corrected? If so, Copernicus, Galileo, Newton, Darwin, and Einstein were "sour revisionists."

When we read Noonan complaining that this view of American history "omits a salient truth: those seeking justice over the years were lucky enough to be operating in a country that had not only a Constitution, but a conscience, to which an appeal could be made. This is a triumph of idealism that is forever a tribute to the human spirit." Again, in the abstract, this sounds fine. But there are some who would not have thought themselves so lucky—not the Scottsboro boy who was lynched; not the Native Americans who were run off their land; not the innumerable nameless victims of racial prejudice whose sufferings find no voice in American history. To espouse these "ideals" without recognizing the disparity between the rhetoric of these claims and the reality of history is to indulge in the most callous form of whitewash.

"Whites," "blacks," "reds," "yellows," and "browns" should all be against the hypocrisy of whitewash. Our national solidarity will be the stronger if it comprises masses of wildly diverse individuals: the solidarity consisting of masses of individuals exactly like each other, cookie-cutter clones of a conformist model, is itself an abnegation of individuality, an invitation to tyrants and demagogues who look for goose-stepping precision in national parades.

I began this chapter with the biblical story of Joseph, and I considered the parallels to the myth of white America. In a sense, Joseph represents the fortunate sibling, the one who is blessed with natural ability, given precious opportunity, and empowered with status and authority. In that sense, every one of the brothers would like to be Joseph, the favorite not only of his father but of the Supreme Father as well. Which minority would not like to attain the status of the white majority in America? If white is the symbol of empowerment, who would not like to be white? But if white is to be properly understood, it cannot be the white of white lies or the white of whitewash; it must be the white that physics identifies for us, the white of many colors. If we understand white in this way, then a coat of white is exactly what this country needs.

I am using the Joseph story as a parable, not as a symbol. It is merely an analogy enabling us to think through some of the situational dilemmas that we face and to understand some of the complex psychologies involved. I am by no means suggesting that the United States is favored of the Almighty or that Americans are the chosen people. Joseph, after all, is a patriarch of the Jews, who may have regarded themselves as the chosen people, but whose lot in history, especially in the twentieth century, has been anything but lucky. Each language, each culture, has a tendency to see itself as the center of the universe, whether it's the Greeks, who regarded all non-Greeks as barbarians, or the Chinese, who saw their country as the "central kingdom." When such a highly civilized culture as Germany in the early twentieth century can spawn National Socialism, we can no longer take it for granted that civilization and barbarism are mutually exclusive. We now realize that there are not only "barbarians within"; there are also "nobles without."

As an analogy, comparing the United States to Joseph does make a certain amount of sense. The United States is literally the most attractive country on earth: we attract more immigrants than any other country. (Japan, by contrast, attracts few immigrants—despite its economic power.) We are the most blessed country in the world—blessed with natural resources, blessed with its favorable place in history, blessed with the richness of its human resources, drawn from every corner of the world. America is Joseph, and it has been favored, more than any other country, with a coat of many colors. This white America must never forget its colorful history.

The United States is a crazy quilt of cultures; its energy, its verve, its good nature, its imagination, its daring, have attracted people from all over the world. Every American is either an immigrant or descended from immigrants: even the Native American probably migrated to the Western hemisphere from Asia. The essence of being American is neither racial nor cultural nor political: those who seek a common thread overlook the most obvious—cultural exiles unified by the belief in the ultimate worth of each individual and the conviction that our strength as a country lies precisely in the diversity of its citizens. The United States—note the plural singular—is a collective unity. A pluralistic one. *E pluribus unum* (out of many, one); *e pluribus pigmentis album* (out of many colors, white). In more than one sense, America is a family *album* of many colors, creeds, and faiths.

". . . *Unum*"

I n speaking of the multicultural dimensions of American culture, we—both those of us who are ethnic and those who think we aren't—need to remind ourselves of the cultural richness inherent in this country. In 1776, we declared our independence as a nation from Great Britain, yet, more than two hundred years later, we seem not to have learned the cultural lesson that political independence has taught us. There are some among us who still think of the United States of America as a cultural offshoot, a backwater of Great Britain. We cannot forget that more than two-thirds of this country was under French or Spanish dominion before it became the United States. Before 1803 and the Louisiana Purchase, most of the lands west of the Mississippi were under French sovereignty; before 1819, Florida was largely Spanish speaking; and, before 1848 and the Mexican Cession, California, Nevada, Utah, most of Arizona, and parts of New Mexico and Colorado were part of Mexico. We need to remember our history before we resent the growing Latino/Latina populations in Florida and California, for these regions are merely returning to their historical roots.

But we would be wrong to conceive of the multicultural character of American culture as merely historical, a thing of the past. The émigrés from Europe and Asia during the Second World War left an indelible mark on American society. (Isn't it interesting that white-collar exiles from abroad are called *émigrés*—not *immigrants?*) Where would America's space program be without Werner von Braun, a German immigrant; where would the development of the hydrogen bomb be without Edward Teller, a Hungarian immigrant? Where would nuclear physics in the United States be without Enrico Fermi, an Italian immigrant? I have counted the number of American Nobel Prize winners from 1950 to 1985 in physics, chemistry, medicine and physiology, and economics: out of 229 prizes won, ninety-nine were awarded to Americans; another twenty-five awardees came to the United States from another country, and became American citizens, most of them after they won the Nobel Prize. In other words, native-born Americans account for 43 percent of the Nobel Prizes awarded in this period, whereas American immigrants account for more than 10 percent. If we add the native-born to the immigrant Americans who have won Nobel prizes, we come up with a total of 124 from 1950 to 1985: one-fifth, or 20 percent, of these Nobel laureates would be immigrants. Compare this to the percentage of American immigrants in the total population of the United States; in 1980, there were 14,080,000 foreign-born residents of the United States, in a population of 226,546,805, or 6.2 percent. In other words, 6.2 percent of Americans have won 20 percent of its Nobel Prizes. One might suggest that, if one measures productivity in terms of Nobel prizes in physics, chemistry, medicine and physiology, and economics, American immigrants are three times as productive as nonimmigrant Americans![1]

---

1. There has been an increase in the proportion of foreign-born residents of the United States. In 1990, the last year for which figures are available, there were 21,632,000 residents who were foreign born in a population of 248,709,873, which constitutes 8.6 percent—an increase of 2.4 percent since 1980. It would be interesting to see if the increase in foreign-born residents is reflected in a higher incidence of U.S. Nobel Prize winners in the years following 1985.

This immigrant contribution to American progress continues. George Gilder's book *Microcosms* (1989) charts the next revolution in technology, which he characterizes as the era in which, via miniaturization and the silicon chip, we can achieve the triumph of "mind over matter." In 1956, as Gilder describes it, "a dark, curly-haired teenager" named Anders Graf was fleeing his native Hungary into Austria. That immigrant—almost a generation later—is now named Andrew Grove, and he is president of Intel, the semiconductor giant. This immigrant depended on other immigrants for growth in the company. "Perhaps half of the key contributors to Intel's success," Gilder reports, "came to the company from foreign countries. Israelis, Chinese, Greeks, Italians, Japanese all played parts in launching the crucial metal oxide silicon and memory technologies that would change the world." The history of modern technology is virtually a roll call of immigrant names: Edmund Cheng, a Chinese-American, was a key figure in Silicon Compilers, Inc.; the major company manufacturing a new storage device for computers, a non-volatile RAM called E-square (for electrically erasable programmable read-only memory) is an Israeli immigrant named Ralph Klein; a young Italian immigrant named Federico Faggin created a "polysilicon" for the controlling gate of a field effect transistor, thus eliminating all use of metals from transistors; an Egyptian immigrant, Amr Mohsen, developed a system for desktop printing of computer chips; the leading pioneer in parallel processing is a company founded by Steven Chen, a Chinese-American, who designed the best-selling supercomputer, the Cray XMP.

Gilder cites over and over again the importance of the immigrants in the history of technological revolution:

> The United States already depends on immigrants for its most
> productive manpower. In fact, even black immigrant families
> are 50 percent more likely than native whites to earn more

than $35,000 a year. By attracting labor and capital, a nation can increase its wealth and power far more effectively than by capturing them or piling up surpluses in mercantilist trade. A key to competition in the global economy will be who wins the hundreds of thousands of skilled workers and entrepreneurs now leaving Hong Kong. (1989, 370).

The competition in the future, Gilders predicts, will be for immigrants: "The chief source of the new wealth of nations is free immigrants. . . . Today, nations have to earn power by attracting immigrants and by liberating their people, their workers and their entrepreneurs" (1989, 369). Yet there will always be an element of society, particularly in economically depressed times, who will vent their frustrations on the newest set of immigrants (past immigrants are lionized but new immigrants anathematized). As the song said, "We used to welcome strangers here." What would America be if it was inhospitable to immigrants, if it were unattractive to immigrants?

If the rainbow has been part of America's neglected past, and if it is the unrecognized backdrop for America's present, it will also be a critical part of America's future. Indeed, one could say that the greatness of America has depended and will always depend on the quality of its immigrants. These immigrants bring their culture, their language, which is no less our language, no less the language of American citizens than English is. In this sense, as I have said, there are no "foreign" languages in the United States. For the native languages of American citizens, particularly its so-called naturalized citizens, constitute virtually all the languages of the world. The multicultural rainbow is in America's past, present, and future. The rainbow is no sentimental symbol: it is the American reality.

Solution to the
Blind Man's Puzzle

The solution is a matter of deduction: it is, of course, crucial that the blind man is asked last. The first person—let's call him A—doesn't know, which eliminates the possibility that the second person—let's call him B—and the blind man both have red hats since that would mean that only blue hats would be left and A could thereby deduce that the hat on his own head must be blue (deduction #1). So A's not knowing suggests that, between B and the blind man, three possibilities remain: both hats are blue; B's hat is red and the blind man's blue; or B's hat is blue and the blind man's red. Each of these possibilities allows for the color of the hat on A to be either red or blue—which is why he doesn't know. Let's turn to B: B cannot be seeing both A and the blind man with red hats, or he would know, just as A would have, that his own hat must be blue (deduction 2). When B indicates in turn that he doesn't know, this reduces these remaining possibilities even further: Now we can assume that, since B also knew the remaining possibilities determined by A's answer, that he, B, and the blind man cannot both have red hats (deduction 1), B would figure out that, if the blind man had a red hat, he, B, must have a blue hat (deduction 3). But B doesn't know, so this possibility—that the blind man has a red hat when B has a blue hat—is eliminated. Of the three possibilities that remain after A indicated that he didn't know—

(1) that B and the blind man both had blue hats; (2) that B had a red hat and the blind man had a blue hat; and (3) that B had a blue hat and the blind man had a red hat—we can eliminate the third option since we have already deduced that, if the blind man had a red hat, B would know that the hat on his head was blue (deduction 3); B's own hat couldn't have been red as well, or else A would have been able to answer the question in the first place (deduction 1). You will note that in the remaining options—(1) that B and the blind man both have blue hats and (2) that B has the red hat and the blind man has the blue hat—B could have a blue or a red hat, depending on the option, which is why he doesn't know. However, the blind man has a blue hat in either option, whatever the color of B's hat. Therefore, the blind man concludes, the hat on his own head is blue.

Works Cited

Abrams, M. H. 1958. *The Mirror and the Lamp*. New York: Norton.

Baring-Gould, William S., and Cecil Baring-Gould, eds. 1962. *The Annotated Mother Goose*. New York: Bramhall.

Brown, H. Douglas. 1980. *Principles of Language Learning and Teaching*. Englewood Cliffs, N.J.: Prentice-Hall.

Coles, William. 1978. *The Plural I: The Teaching of Writing*. New York: Holt, Rinehart & Winston.

Coulmas, Florian, ed. 1981. *A Festschrift for Native Speaker*. The Hague: Mouton.

Dickens, Charles. 1963. *Great Expectations*. New York: Signet.

Donne, John. 1959. *Devotions upon Emergent Occasions*. Ann Arbor: University of Michigan Press.

Emerson, Ralph Waldo. 1904. *Society and Solitude*. Boston: Houghton Mifflin.

Estrada, Susan. 1993. *Connecting to the Internet: A Buyer's Guide*. Sebastopol, Calif.: O'Reilly.

Feldman, David. 1987. *Why Do Clocks Run Clockwise? and Other Imponderables*. New York: Harper & Row.

Ferguson, Charles, and Shirley Brice Heath. eds. 1981. *Language in the USA*. Cambridge: Cambridge University Press.

Fishman, Joshua. 1966. *Language Loyalty in the United States.* The Hague: Mouton.

Furuyama, Francis. 1989. "End of History." *National Interest* 16 (Summer): 3–18.

Gabler, Neal. 1988. *An Empire of Their Own: How the Jews Invented Hollywood.* New York: Anchor.

Gilder, George. 1989. *Microcosms: The Quantum Revolution in Economics and Technology.* New York: Simon & Schuster.

Glazer, Nathan, and Daniel P. Moynihan. 1963. *Beyond the Melting Pot.* Cambridge, Mass.: MIT Press and Harvard University Press.

Goleman, Daniel. 1987. "The Mind over the Body." *New York Times Magazine*, 27 September, 36ff.

Griffin, John Howard. 1961. *Black like Me.* Boston: Houghton Mifflin.

Hardin, C. L. 1988. *Color for Philosophers: Unweaving the Rainbow.* Indianapolis: Hackett.

Harris, Joseph. 1987. "The Plural Text/The Plural Self: Roland Barthes and William Coles." *College English* 49, no. 2 (February): 158–70.

Havelock, Eric A. 1986. *The Muse Learns to Write.* New Haven, Conn.: Yale University Press.

Herrl, George. 1965. *Carl P. Dietz Collection of Typewriters.* Publications in History no. 7. Milwaukee: Milwaukee Public Museum.

Kuhn, Thomas. 1962. *The Structure of Scientific Revolutions.* Chicago: University of Chicago Press.

Lamb, W. R. M., trans. 1946. *Plato, with an English Translation.* Cambridge, Mass.: Harvard University Press.

Lau, D. C., trans. 1970. *Mencius*. Harmondsworth: Penguin.

Lewis, Bernard. 1973. *Islam in History*. New York: The Library.

Lienhardt, Godfrey. 1961. *Divinity and Experience: The Religion of the Dinka*. Oxford: Clarendon.

Logan, Robert K. 1986. *The Alphabet Effect*. New York: Morrow.

Mill, John Stuart. 1947. *On Liberty*. New York: Appleton-Century-Crofts.

Milton, John. 1959. *The Complete Prose Works of John Milton*. New Haven, Conn.: Yale University Press.

Needham, Joseph. 1954–. *Science and Civilization in China*. 6 vols. Cambridge: Cambridge University Press.

Nida, Eugene. 1966. "On Bible Translating." In *On Translation*, ed. Reuben Brower. Cambridge, Mass.: Harvard University Press, 1959; Oxford: Oxford University Press.

Noonan, Peggy. 1991. "Why the World Comes Here." *Reader's Digest*, July, 39–42.

Paikeday, Thomas. 1985. *The Native Speaker is Dead!* Toronto: Paikeday.

Pepper, Stephen. 1942. *World Hypotheses: A Study in Evidence*. Berkeley: University of California Press.

The Real Mother Goose. [1916] 1944. Chicago: Rand-McNally.

Reich, Robert. 1990. "Who Is 'Us'?" *Harvard Business Review* 68, no. 1 (January–February): 53–64.

Rodriguez, Richard. 1989. "An American Writer." In *The Invention of Ethnicity*, ed. Werner Sollors. New York: Oxford University Press.

Sagarin, Edward, and Robert J. Kelly. 1985. "Polylingualism in the United States of America: A Multitude of Tones amid a Monolingual Majority." In *Language Policy and National Unity*, eds. William R. Beer and James E. Jacob. Totowa, N.J.: Rowman and Allanheld.

Scarry, Richard. [1964] 1970. *Best Mother Goose Ever.* New York: Golden Books.

The Sesame Street Players Present Mother Goose. 1980. New York: Random House.

Shih, Vincent Yu-chung, trans. 1983. *The Literary Mind and the Carving of Dragons.* Hong Kong: University of Hong Kong Press.

Simon, Paul. 1980. *The Tongue-tied American.* New York: Continuum.

Sollors, Werner. 1986. *Beyond Ethnicity: Consent and Descent in American Culture.* New York: Oxford University Press.

Speiser, E. A. 1964. *The Anchor Bible: Genesis.* Garden City, N.Y.: Doubleday.

Steele, Shelby. 1990. *The Content of Our Character.* New York: St. Martin's.

The Tall Book of Mother Goose. 1943. New York: Harper.

Terkel, Studs. 1980. *American Dreams: Lost and Found.* New York: Pantheon.

Time. Autumn (special issue), 1993. "The New Face of America: How Immigrants Are Shaping the World's First Multicultural Society."

Tuan, Yi-fu. 1982. *Segmented Worlds and Self: Group Life and Individual Consciousness.* Minneapolis: University of Minnesota Press.

Ugwu-Ohu, Dympna. 1993. "Hers." *New York Times Magazine,* 14 November, 40–41.

Waley, Arthur, trans. 1960. *Tale of Genji*. New York: Random House.

Watson, Burton, trans. 1961. *Records of the Grand Historian*, by Ssu-ma Ch'ien [Sima Qian]. 2 vols. New York: Columbia University Press.

Watson, Burton, trans. 1968. *The Complete Works of Chuang Tzu*. New York: Columbia University Press.

Wriston, Walter. 1992. *The Twilight of Soveriegnty*. New York: Scribner's.

Zukav, Gary. 1979. *The Dancing Wu-li Masters: An Overview of the New Physics*. New York: William Morrow.

Index